QUEEN ELIZABETH II
A DIAMOND JUBILEE SOUVENIR ALBUM

JANE ROBERTS

ROYAL COLLECTION PUBLICATIONS

2012 marks the Diamond Jubilee of the accession to the throne of Princess Elizabeth, on the death of her father King George VI in early 1952. Queen Elizabeth II is only the second British monarch to have achieved this anniversary, following in the footsteps of her great-great-grandmother, Queen Victoria (reigned 1837–1901).

Her Majesty The Queen ascended the throne at the age of 25. Four years before, she had married her third cousin, Prince Philip, Duke of Edinburgh. The eldest of their four children – Charles and Anne – were born in 1948 and 1950 respectively. In the following pages The Queen's family and key events in her remarkable life and reign are illustrated, together with the exceptional leadership that she has provided to her country and Commonwealth, over six decades. Happy and Glorious, Long May She Reign!

The official photograph of Queen Victoria issued for her Diamond Jubilee in 1897 had been taken four years earlier. It shows the Queen swathed in her wedding lace, wearing a Garter sash and star, with diamond necklace and earrings. She wears the small crown (shown below, with its arches) made in 1870 after she had resolved not to wear the Imperial State Crown again, following the death of her beloved Prince Albert, in 1861.

Queen Victoria was 78 in the year of her Diamond Jubilee, and had also been Empress of India since 1871. In the Diamond Jubilee year of Queen Elizabeth II, Her Majesty will celebrate her eighty-sixth birthday.

One of the most significant changes of the last sixty or so years has been the gradual transition from Empire to Commonwealth. The future Queen was indeed 'our Empire's Little Princess' when the teacup and saucer (shown opposite) were produced in the late 1920s, but her father ceased to be Emperor when India became independent in 1947.

Ten years later the same photographer, Marcus Adams, was commissioned to record the new Royal Family, resulting in the photograph below, taken four days after the accession of the Princess's father as King George VI, following the abdication of King Edward VIII. That event was to change the Princess's life for ever.

Among other notable differences between the United Kingdom in 1897 and in 2012 is the increasingly widespread availability of photographic images, and of international travel. This tiny leather frame contains photographs of the seven-month-old Princess Elizabeth, taken in December 1926. Soon afterwards her parents took it on their six-month tour of Australia and New Zealand in 1927.

1926

Her Majesty Queen Elizabeth II was born on
21 April 1926 at No. 17 Bruton Street, the
London home of her maternal grandparents,
the Earl and Countess of Strathmore.

She was the first child of the Duke of York
(known to his family as 'Bertie'),
King George V's second son, and his wife,
formerly Lady Elizabeth Bowes Lyon.

The first photographs of Princess Elizabeth were taken in May, shortly before her christening at Buckingham Palace. The christening group shows the infant Princess in her mother's arms, with her father standing behind (second from right). Her maternal grandmother, the Countess of Strathmore, is seated to right of centre. Princess Elizabeth's godparents were her paternal grandparents, King George V and Queen Mary (both second from left); her maternal grandfather, the Earl of Strathmore (back right), her aunts Princess Mary, Viscountess Lascelles (front right), and Lady Elphinstone (front left); and her great-great uncle, the Duke of Connaught (back left).

The Duke of Connaught's christening present to his great-great niece was this magnificent silver cup.

1927

During much of the six-month overseas tour carried out by the Duke and Duchess of York in the first half of 1927, Princess Elizabeth was looked after by her grandparents, spending time at both Buckingham Palace and the Strathmores' Hertfordshire home, St Paul's Walden Bury.

The photograph above of the smiling Princess in her pram was among those sent to the Duchess of York by Lady Strathmore, to record the baby's progress.

The Queen has been photographed by passers-by, and by professional photographers, throughout her long life. The fleeting record of her pushing her dolls' pram in Piccadilly contrasts with the engaging image of the two-year-old Princess taken by Marcus Adams in his studio in July 1928.

This is one of Princess Elizabeth's dolls.

1929

Princess Elizabeth's father was a keen amateur photographer and his snapshots of his infant daughter speak fondly of his regard for her. The photograph with the lilies was taken at St Paul's Walden Bury, the Hertfordshire home of the Earl and Countess of Strathmore. It was exhibited by the future King at the 1930 Kodak exhibition.

This detail of Princess Elizabeth with an umbrella is from a photograph taken by her father in 1928.

1930

Queen Mary greatly enjoyed the company of her eldest granddaughter, who accompanied her to the Naval and Military Tournament at Olympia, London, in May 1930.

The first London home of the Duke and Duchess of York, and of Princess Elizabeth, was No. 145 Piccadilly, destroyed during the Second World War. The tiny Princess is here shown in a horse-drawn landau outside the front door.

Lilibet's first letter to me

HER MAJESTY
THE QUEEN.

145 PICCADILLY
W.1.

DARLING GRANNY.
I THANK YOU VERY
VERY MUCH FOR
THE LOVELY DOLL'S
HOUSE. I DO LOVE
IT, AND I HAVE
UNPACKED THE

145 PICCADILLY
W.1.

DINING ROOM AND
THE HALL.
LOVE FROM
LILIBET.
XXX

In 1931 the Princess wrote her first letter to Queen Mary, by which time she was confidently riding her tricycle in the park.

The family spent part of the summer of 1931 at Glamis, the Strathmores' Scottish seat. The poise of the 5-year-old Princess is clear from her conversation with the Dowager Countess of Airlie, who was her senior by sixty years.

1932

The day nursery at St Paul's Walden Bury contained a much-loved rocking horse. Here Princess Elizabeth shares a ride with her younger sister, Princess Margaret, born in 1930. Their mother had played with the same rocking horse as a child.

Princess Elizabeth enjoyed riding from an early age and was given her first pony when she was 4 years old. By 1932 she was riding on her own.

1933

1933

The oil painting of Princess Elizabeth on the previous page was commissioned by her father, the Duke of York, as a gift for her mother. It was painted in 1933 by the Hungarian artist Philip de László. Sittings took place at Royal Lodge, the country home of the Duke and Duchess of York in Windsor Great Park. In the right background is the diminutive figure of the Copper Horse, which could be seen through the window.

The photograph on this page was taken by Princess Victoria, King George V's sister, outside the little Welsh Cottage – Y Bwthyn Bach – in the grounds of Royal Lodge. The cottage had been given to Princess Elizabeth by the people of Wales for her sixth birthday in 1932. The Princess stands alongside her grandparents (the King and Queen), with her mother and little sister to the left.

Fox

16th Feb. 1934.

Dear Granny,

Thank you very much for the lovely little jersey.

We loved staying at Sandringham with you. I lost a top front tooth yesterday morning.

Margaret and I went to a fancy dress party at Lady Astor's. It was simply lovely. There was a clown and a jester and a snowman and lots of people I knew. There were stalls full of lovely things in them. There were lovely flowers and toys and sweets.

Love from
Lilibet

In another letter to Queen Mary, of February 1934, Princess Elizabeth mentions that she has lost a top front tooth. At the end of the same year she was one of the bridesmaids at the wedding of her father's younger brother, the Duke of Kent, where this portrait photograph was taken.

1935

In spite of the four years that separated them, there was a close bond between Princesses Elizabeth and Margaret. They were photographed shopping together (with their mother and grandmother) in Forfar, close to Glamis, in August 1935.

Lilibet. 1935 Margaret

Later that year, the Princesses sent a joint Christmas card – with their names added by 'Lilibet', the elder of the two.

The Hungarian artist Sigismund de Stróbl was professor of sculpture at the Budapest Royal Academy before moving to London. His marble head, completed in 1937, was based on the portrait modelled during visits by Princess Elizabeth to his London studio.

Dogs have always played an important part in the lives of The Queen and her family. Here Princess Elizabeth holds Jane, the second royal corgi to have been acquired by the Duke and Duchess of York. The first one – Dookie – was purchased in 1933.

1937

The Coronation

12th May, 1937.

To Mummy and Papa

In Memory of Their Coronation

From Lilibet
By Herself.

---

①

An Account of the Coronation

At 5 o'clock in the morning I was woken up by the band of the Royal Marines striking up just outside my window. I leapt out of bed and so did Bobo. We put on dressing-gowns and shoes and Bobo made me put on an eiderdown as it was so cold and we crouched in the window looking onto a cold, misty morning. There were already some people in the stands and all the time people were coming to them in a stream with occasional pauses in between.

Every now and then we were hopping in and out of bed looking at the bands and the soldiers.

At six o'clock Bobo got up and instead of getting up at my usual time I jumped out of bed at half-past seven. When I was going to the bathroom I passed the lift as usual, and who should walk out but Miss Daly! I was very pleased to see her. When I was dressed I went into the nursery and Margaret Elphinstone, who

---

②

came to breakfast, was waiting there. We did not eat very much as we were too excited. After we had finished we looked out of the window until it was time to get dressed. We saw the Canadian Mounted Police in their red coats and once when a policeman went by on his bicycle, everybody cheered!

When we were dressed we showed ourselves to the visitors and the housemaids. Now I shall try and give you a description of our dresses. They were white silk with old cream lace and had little gold bows all the way down the middle. They had puffed sleeves with one little bow in the centre. Then there were the robes of purple velvet with gold on the edge.

We went along to Mummy's bedroom and we found her putting on her dress. Papa was dressed in a white shirt, breeches and stockings, and over this he wore a crimson satin coat. Then a page came and said it was time

---

③

to go down, so we kissed Mummy, and wished her good luck and went down. There we said 'good morning' to Aunt Alice, Aunt Marina and Aunt Mary with whom we were to drive to the Abbey. We were then told to get into the carriage. When we got in we still had to wait a few minutes and then our carriage moved from the door. At first it was very jolty but we soon got used to it. We went round the Memorial, down the Mall, through Admiralty Arch, along Whitehall, past the Cenotaph and the Horse Guards' Parade, and then Westminster Abbey. When we got out we were welcomed by the Duke of Norfolk, the Earl Marshal.

We waited in the little dressing-room until it was time to go up the aisle. Then we arranged ourselves to form the procession. First of all came two Heralds, then two Gentleman Ushers, then all in a line, Margaret, Aunt Mary and myself. When we got to the Theatre we sat down and waited for Queen

---

④

Mary's procession. Grannie looked too beautiful in a gold dress patterned with golden flowers. Then we went up the steps and into the box. There we sat down and waited for about half-an-hour until Mummy's procession began. Then came Papa looking very beautiful in a crimson robe and the Cap of State. Then the service began.

I thought it all very, very wonderful and I expect the Abbey did, too. The arches and beams at the top were covered with a sort of haze of wonder as Papa was crowned, at least I thought so.

When Mummy was crowned and all the peeresses put on their coronets it looked wonderful to see arms and coronets hovering in the air and then the arms disappeared as if by magic. Also the music was lovely and the band, the orchestra and the new organ all played beautifully.

---

⑤

What struck me as being rather odd was that Grannie did not remember much of her own Coronation. I should have thought that it would have stayed in her mind for ever.

At the end the service got rather boring as it was all prayers. Grannie and I were looking to see how many more pages to the end, and we turned one more and then I pointed to the word at the bottom of the page and it said "Finis". We both smiled at each other and turned back to the service.

After Papa had passed we were all shivering because there was a most awful draught coming from somewhere, so we were glad to get out of the box. Then we went down the aisle, first a gentleman I did not know, then Margaret and myself and then Grannie. When we got back to our dressing-room we had some sandwiches, stuffed rolls, orangeade and lemonade. Then we left for our

---

long drive.

On leaving the Abbey we went along the Embankment, Northumberland Avenue, through Trafalgar, St. James's St., Piccadilly, Regent St., Oxford St. with Selfridge's lovely figures, through Marble Arch, through Hyde Park, Hyde Park Corner, Constitution Hill, round the Memorial and into the courtyard.

Then we went up to the corridor to see the Coach coming in. Then Mummy and Papa came up and said "Good morning" and were congratulated. Then we all went on to the Balcony where millions of people were waiting below. After that we all went to be photographed in front of those awful lights.

When we sat down to tea it was nearly six o'clock! When I got into bed my legs ached terribly. As my head touched the pillow I was asleep and I did not wake up till nearly eight o'clock the next morning.

The death of King George V in January 1936, followed by the abdication of King Edward VIII in December of the same year, led to the accession of the Duke of York as King George VI. He was crowned at Westminster Abbey on 12 May 1937 – the date previously fixed for King Edward VIII's coronation. Princess Elizabeth, now heir to the British throne, wrote a full account of the ceremony in a lined exercise book, concluding that it was '<u>very</u>, <u>very</u> wonderful'. After the service the Princesses were photographed with their parents in the Throne Room at Buckingham Palace, wearing the gold coronets made for the occasion.

1938

'France' and 'Marianne' were made in France for Princess Elizabeth and Princess Margaret in 1938. With their magnificent wardrobes, supplied by Parisian houses such as Lanvin, Worth, Hermès and Cartier, they were presented by Charles Corbin, French Ambassador in London, as described in a letter to Queen Mary. A temporary public display of the dolls (which were clearly not to be played with) was soon arranged at St James's Palace, in aid of the newly renamed Princess Elizabeth of York Hospital for Children. The dolls are now on view at Windsor Castle.

BUCKINGHAM PALACE

15th Nov. 1938.

Darling Grannie,

Thank you very much for the lovely brooch. How clever that lady must be to make it out of a penny. It is very like Grandpapa.

What a horrible day for driving in a carriage and it must be very foggy in the

BUCKINGHAM PALACE

Channel.

M. Corbin came yesterday to hand over the dolls on behalf of the French people and we showed him all their clothes.

Thank you very much again

Your loving granddaughter

Lilibet

MARIANNE

27th March.
1939.

BUCKINGHAM PALACE

Darling Grannie,
          I am very sorry to
hear that you have a sore throat.
I do hope it will not develope into
influenza. That would be a great
bore during this cold spell of
weather.
          We had one of the coldest week-
ends we have had this winter at
Royal Lodge this time. It was
icy.
          We have begun riding in the
riding-school here and we are
learning to jump which is great fun

BUCKINGHAM PALACE

          I expect we will be seeing you
at Windsor soon, it does come round
so quickly and to think I am
already going to be thirteen.
          I do hope you will get better
very quickly and be able to go
about again.
          Your very loving grand-daughter,
                    Lilibet

The diligent and affectionate
correspondence with Queen
Mary continued with this
letter in which the Princess
looks forward to seeing her
grandmother at Windsor,
adding 'to think I am already
going to be thirteen'.

Princess Elizabeth's thirteenth birthday was
spent at Royal Lodge in Windsor Great Park
and was marked by a charming photograph of
the King riding with his two daughters. The
saddle used by Princess Elizabeth at this time
has remained at Windsor.

1940

A Message from
Princess Elizabeth
to British Children Abroad

IN WISHING YOU ALL GOOD EVEN ∕ ing, I feel that I am speaking to friends and companions who have shared with my sister and myself many a happy children's hour. Thousands of you in this country have had to leave your homes and be separated from your fathers and mothers. My sister Margaret Rose and I feel so much for you, as we

On 12 October 1940, just over a year after the outbreak of war, the 14-year-old Princess Elizabeth made her first radio broadcast, to the children of Britain and the Empire, as part of the BBC's *Children's Hour* programme. A miniature printed transcript of the broadcast text was subsequently published in New York, and a specially bound version was presented to the King and Queen.

This photograph of the Princesses working on their vegetable plot at Royal Lodge, with corgi in attendance, shows something of the relatively carefree life which they were able to enjoy away from London. While the King and Queen remained at Buckingham Palace during the week, the Princesses spent much of the war years at Windsor.

The platinum and diamond basket brooch, set with rubies, Indian emeralds and sapphires, was given to Princess Elizabeth by her parents in 1941.

1942

Like all British subjects, Princess Elizabeth's life was subject to wartime legislation. She was required to carry an identity card at all times, and to use ration books to obtain food and clothing.

The Princess – wearing her Girl Guide uniform – was photographed on 5 May 1942 signing her registration documents. Her ration books and identity card have survived in the Royal Archives.

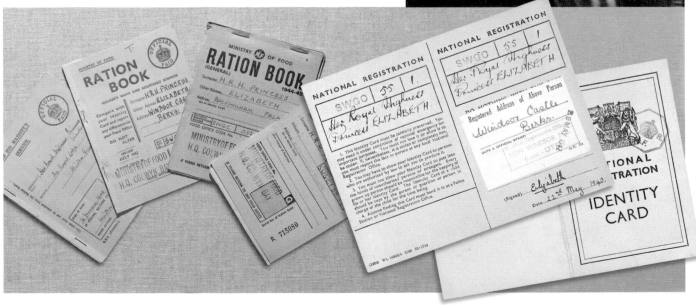

PROGRAMME

OF

Christmas Pantomime

ALADDIN

IN THE

WATERLOO CHAMBER
WINDSOR CASTLE

DECEMBER 16th, 17th and 18th, 1943

PRICE 1s.

ALADDIN

CHARACTERS

Aladdin	.. ..	PRINCESS ELIZABETH
Princess Roxana	.. .. ..	PRINCESS MARGARET
Widow Twankey	.. .. ..	CYRIL WOODS
Abanazar	.. ..	JAMES COX
Sing Lo	.. ..	MAUREEN SIDDLE
Sing Hi	.. ..	RENE HELPS
Ping Ho	.. .. ..	KENNETH RICHARDSON
Pong Ho	.. .. ..	GEORGE PRATLEY
Strolling Player	.. .. ..	CORPORAL BRAZMAN *(The Life Guards)*

CHORUS

ORCHESTRA OF THE ROYAL HORSE GUARDS ("THE BLUES")
(under the direction of Captain J. A. Hochhauffen)

Written and produced by H. L. Tanner

Scenes by J. M. Mereghes

Act I Scene 1
A Street in Peking

Act I Scene 2
The Teashop of the Willow Pattern Plate

Act II Scene 1
Widow Twankey's Laundry

Act III Scene 1
The Ruby Cave

Act III Scene 2
The Emperor's Palace

Aladdin was the Christmas entertainment at Windsor in 1943. Princesses Elizabeth and Margaret headed the cast, and appear in the group photograph at either side of the Headmaster of the Royal School at Windsor, who wrote and produced the pantomime. This was one of many pantomimes staged in the Waterloo Chamber during the war years. Tickets were sold in aid of the Wool Fund – which supplied knitting wool for the making of comforters for members of the armed forces.

"ALADDIN"
Windsor Castle. Christmas, 1943
Elizabeth   Margaret

1944

On her eighteenth birthday Princess Elizabeth
was presented with the Colonel's Colour of
the Grenadier Guards in the Quadrangle at
Windsor Castle. She had been appointed
Colonel of the regiment two years before, on
her sixteenth birthday. In 1952, when The
Queen became Colonel-in-Chief of all the
Household regiments, this Colour was placed
in the Queen's Guard Chamber, where
it remains on view to this day.

Among Princess Elizabeth's eighteenth
birthday presents from the King and Queen
was this linked bracelet by Cartier.

The first Royal Windsor Horse Show took
place in 1944. Princess Elizabeth won this
silver cup for 'The best turn out not
exceeding 13 hands' in the
Private Driving class.

1945

Princess Elizabeth joined the Auxiliary Territorial Service (the ATS) early in 1945, when she was registered as No. 230873 Second Subaltern Elizabeth Alexandra Mary Windsor. After undertaking a driving and vehicle maintenance course at Aldershot, she qualified on 14 April, just before her nineteenth birthday. Three months later she was promoted to Junior Commander.

After the declaration of peace in May 1945, Princess Elizabeth was able to travel more widely and undertook a broader range of duties. In March 1946 she launched the new aircraft carrier HMS *Eagle* at the Harland & Wolff shipyard in Belfast. Five months later she was invested as a bard, with the title 'Elizabeth o Windsor', at the annual National Eisteddfod of Wales.

1947

In February 1947 Princess Elizabeth joined the King and Queen and Princess Margaret for the royal tour of South Africa. They travelled out on HMS *Vanguard*, where the ship's cat clearly enjoyed the Princesses' company. In South Africa the longer journeys were undertaken on the Royal Train. A press photographer captured the Princess's delight at sounding the train's whistle.

While the Royal Family was in South Africa, Princess Elizabeth celebrated her twenty-first birthday. The Government of South Africa presented her with a necklace made of twenty-one magnificent diamonds. After the accession the necklace was shortened and the diamonds which had been removed were made into a bracelet.

ON the Coming MARRIAGE of HER ROYAL HIGHNESS, the PRINCESS ELIZABETH

WHAT IS THE CROWN
but something set above
The jangle and the jargon and the hate
Of strivers after power in the State,
A symbol, like a banner, for mens' love?

When hope is dim and luck is out of joint,
when enemies within, without, assail,
where a Crown shines, the courage cannot fail,
There a land's spirit finds a rallying-point.

On 10 July 1947 the engagement was announced between Princess Elizabeth and her third cousin, Lieutenant Philip Mountbatten (born Prince Philip of Greece). The platinum and diamond engagement ring was made using stones from a tiara that had belonged to the bridegroom's mother. The engagement was celebrated in a poem by the Poet Laureate, John Masefield.

1947

The bride's wedding dress was designed by Norman Hartnell. The 15-foot star-patterned train was woven in Braintree, Essex, and incorporated symbols of rebirth and growth.

Princess Elizabeth wore her mother's diamond tiara. The pearl and diamond earrings had been a twenty-first birthday present from her grandmother, Queen Mary.

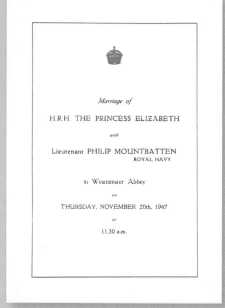

Marriage of

H.R.H. THE PRINCESS ELIZABETH

with

Lieutenant PHILIP MOUNTBATTEN
ROYAL NAVY

In Westminster Abbey

on

THURSDAY, NOVEMBER 20th, 1947

at

11.30 a.m.

The Princess's wedding took place at Westminster Abbey on 20 November 1947. It provided a moment of joy and celebration amidst the difficult years of national recovery following the end of the war. The bridegroom was created HRH The Duke of Edinburgh shortly before the wedding. Following her marriage, Princess Elizabeth was also known as The Duchess of Edinburgh.

1947

The religious service was followed by a Wedding Breakfast at Buckingham Palace. This tiny silver-painted shoe was part of the decoration of one of the Princess's wedding cakes.

The honeymoon was spent at Broadlands in Hampshire, the home of Prince Philip's uncle, Lord Mountbatten. Sixty years later, The Queen and Prince Philip returned to Broadlands to be photographed in the same poses. The Queen wore the same jewellery in 2007 as in 1947.

Princess Elizabeth's first child, Prince Charles, was born at Buckingham Palace on 14 November 1948. A hand-written announcement of his birth, signed by the royal doctors, was hung on the palace railings.

The King and Queen gave their daughter this flower basket brooch to celebrate the new arrival. Princess Elizabeth is shown wearing the brooch in the first photographs of mother and child, taken by Cecil Beaton in mid-December.

1949

The Duke of Edinburgh resumed his naval career after his marriage. In October 1949 he was appointed second-in-command of HMS *Chequers*, part of the Mediterranean fleet based in Malta. For nearly two years Princess Elizabeth divided her time between Britain and Malta; the royal couple are seen here on the roof of the Villa Guardamangia in Malta. This Maltese lace mat was part of a gift to the Princess from the residents of St Vincent de Paule in 1949.

This magnificent Rolls-Royce Phantom IV was made for Princess Elizabeth and The Duke of Edinburgh in the late 1940s. The detachable mascot on the bonnet – a silver figure of St George and the Dragon – was designed by the artist Edward Seago and remains in use to this day on The Queen's official car.

1950

Princess Elizabeth's second child, Princess Anne, was born on 15 August 1950 at Clarence House, into which her family had moved one year before.

In the month before Princess Anne's birth The Duke of Edinburgh had been promoted to the rank of Lieutenant-Commander.

This elegant dress was made for
one of Princess Elizabeth's
official appearances
at this time.

In October 1951 The Duke of Edinburgh
and Princess Elizabeth embarked on their
first major tour together, to Canada and the
United States. On the last evening of their
stay in Ottawa, the Governor-General gave a
private party in their honour, during which
they took part in a Canadian square dance.

1952

Just two months after their return from North America, the royal couple set off on a Commonwealth tour which was due to take them to Australia and New Zealand, via East Africa and Sri Lanka. News of The King's death on 6 February 1952 reached the royal party at Sagana Lodge, Kenya. The tour was immediately terminated and on 7 February the new Queen was greeted on arrival at London Airport by her Household and Government, including the Prime Minister, Winston Churchill. On the following day she was formally proclaimed Queen.

The Williamson diamond brooch was made for The Queen by Cartier in 1952, as a setting for the 54.5-carat pink diamond she had been given by John T. Williamson as a wedding gift in 1947. The diamond had been discovered in Dr Williamson's mine in Tanganyika in the month before the royal wedding. In 1948 it was cut into a 23.6-carat brilliant in London, and was later set into this jonquil-shaped flower.

At the time of The Queen's accession her family's London residence was Clarence House, where they were shown by the artist Edward Halliday. The Queen and her family moved to Buckingham Palace before the Coronation in the following year.

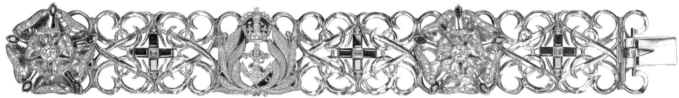

In November 1952 The Queen and Duke of Edinburgh celebrated their fifth wedding anniversary. The Duke's anniversary present was this bracelet, made by Boucheron to The Duke's own design. It includes interlocking Es and Ps, a naval badge set in diamonds, crosses made of rubies and sapphires, and two Roses of York.

Christmas 1952 was spent at Sandringham, where The Queen broadcast her first Christmas message. The tradition of the Christmas broadcast had been begun by her grandfather, King George V, exactly twenty years earlier.

1953

Norman Hartnell

By the start of 1953 preparations for the Coronation, set for 2 June, were well under way. The purple velvet Coronation Robe – the Robe of Estate – was embroidered at the Royal School of Needlework, while the Coronation Dress was designed by Norman Hartnell and made in his London workroom. Its decoration incorporates emblems of both the United Kingdom and the Commonwealth. In 1977 Hartnell – who had also designed and made The Queen's wedding dress – became the first royal couturier to be knighted.

Invitations were issued – including this special one, addressed to Prince Charles – and the processional route was planned. Following the ceremony in Westminster Abbey, the royal procession (which included over 16,000 participants) travelled over 4½ miles (7.2 km) before returning to Buckingham Palace.

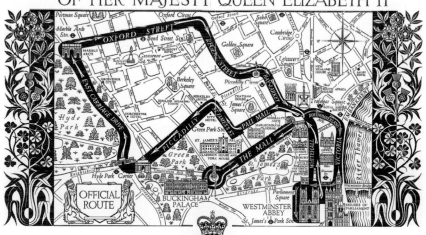

Many souvenirs were created to commemorate the event, including this toy model of the Gold State Coach.

1953

The crowning is the most dramatic moment of the Coronation ceremony. It is a stage in the fourth part of the ceremony – the investiture of the Sovereign with the ornaments that are 'the outward and visible signs of an inward and spiritual grace'. The majority of the regalia used in 1953 had been made for the coronation of Charles II in 1661. Shown here (clockwise, from bottom left) are the Armills, Ampulla, Sovereign's Sceptre with Cross, Sovereign's Sceptre with Dove, St Edward's Staff, St Edward's Crown (used for the crowning), the Sovereign's Orb, and the Spurs. For the 1953 Coronation an additional pair of gold Armills (below), and a new Stole were presented by the Commonwealth.

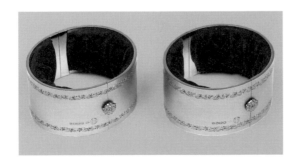

1953

Towards the end of her Coronation Service, The Queen changed into the velvet Coronation Robe and exchanged St Edward's Crown (shown on previous page) for the Imperial State Crown, which she wore for her return to Buckingham Palace (right).

The Queen's Coronation was celebrated throughout the nation and Commonwealth. The first to be televised, it was watched by an estimated twenty million people from their homes. In the evening a firework display lit up the Thames at Westminster.

1954

The Queen's longest-ever tour, to Commonwealth countries in the West Indies, Australasia, Asia and Africa, began in November 1953 and lasted until May 1954. The total distance covered was over 40,000 miles.

This gold lamé and white lace one-shoulder gown was made for the 1953 – 4 royal tour. Like The Queen's Coronation Dress, it was designed by Norman Hartnell. The Coronation Dress was also taken on the tour and was worn in Wellington, Canberra and Colombo.

Early in the tour the Government and People of Australia presented The Queen with a diamond brooch in the form of a sprig of Golden Wattle and a spray of Tea Tree blossom. The visit to Flemington Races, Melbourne, was one of the many occasions on which Her Majesty wore the brooch.

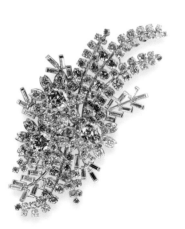

The Order of the Garter, founded in 1348, is the senior British Order of Chivalry. The monarch is Sovereign of the Order and personally appoints new Knights – and Ladies – of the Garter. The Queen was appointed a Lady of the Garter by King George VI in 1947, shortly before her marriage.

In Cecil Beaton's photograph taken in November 1955, The Queen wears her diamond-set Garter Star. This had been a present from the Royal Navy to King George VI in 1923 and was given to Princess Elizabeth by her father at the time of her investiture.

The Queen also wears the diamond-encrusted Marlborough George (above), made for George IV in 1825, suspended from her Garter Collar or chain.

1956

This photograph of the Royal Family on board HMY *Britannia* was taken in 1956. By that time the Royal Yacht had been in active service for over two years. Plans for a new vessel had been announced in October 1951 and *Britannia* was launched by The Queen in April 1953. She was commissioned in January 1954 in time to be used for the final homeward journey, from Malta to London, at the end of the 1953–4 Commonwealth tour. Sir Hugh Casson, who had designed the royal apartments on *Britannia*, included the sketch below in a letter to The Queen.

Anne   Charles

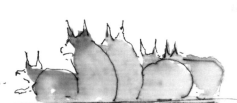

In early 1956 The Queen and Duke of
Edinburgh paid a three-week visit to Nigeria,
in the course of which she addressed the
House of Representatives in Lagos. The
dress worn on that occasion was
designed by Norman Hartnell.

1957

The State Visit to the United States in
October 1957 was the fourth such visit
undertaken by The Queen in a single year.
In New York a traditional ticker-tape
welcome was provided for the royal couple.

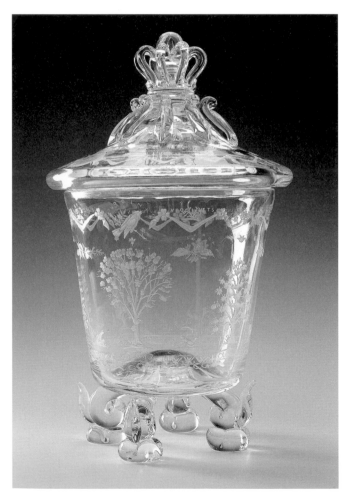

In the course of this visit, The Queen
addressed the United Nations for the first
time. This Steuben glass cup, decorated with
animals, trees and birds native to North
America, was a gift from President Eisenhower.

Each day of her life since February 1952,
The Queen has dealt with her 'boxes' – the
leather-covered cases containing documents
and papers for her attention, forwarded by
her Private Secretary.

1959

The Queen in the Private Dining Room at
Windsor Castle, painted by The Duke of
Edinburgh. The Duke began to paint in
oils in the late 1940s, and was encouraged
and assisted by Edward Seago.

Sugar was the daughter of The Queen's first corgi, Susan, which she had been given in 1944. This portrait of Sugar, drawn in 1957, hangs in The Queen's Sitting Room at Buckingham Palace.

Sugar was a favourite royal companion until her death in 1965 and in 1959 was photographed with The Queen in the grounds of Frogmore House, Windsor.

1960

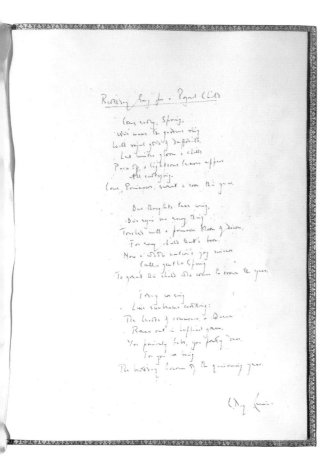

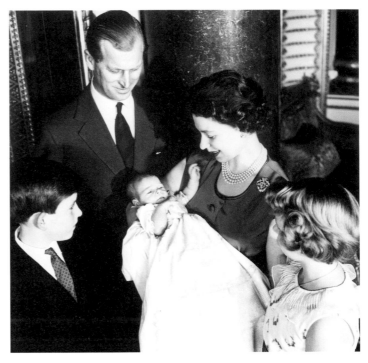

The Queen's second son and third child, Prince Andrew, was born at Buckingham Palace in February 1960. His arrival was celebrated in verse by C. Day-Lewis, who was to become Poet Laureate in 1968, following the death of John Masefield. The 'Birthday Song for a Royal Child' was set to music by Arthur Bliss, Master of The Queen's Music.

In May 1960 Cecil Beaton photographed The Queen dressed for the wedding of Princess Margaret to the photographer Antony Armstrong-Jones (created Earl of Snowdon in 1961). The Queen's dress was another creation of Norman Hartnell. The diamond brooch worn on this occasion is the 'Lover's Knot', inherited by The Queen on Queen Mary's death in 1953.

1961

In the course of her visit, The Queen was honoured with a ceremonial ride on an ornately decorated elephant. In 1939 a press photographer had recorded her enjoying an earlier elephant ride, at London Zoo.

The Queen paid her first visit to the Indian sub-continent in 1961, when she visited India, Pakistan and Nepal. The invitation to President Prasad's banquet in her honour, on the day of her arrival in India, was inscribed on bark and delivered in an elaborately decorated box.

The original cathedral (formerly a parish church) in Coventry had been largely destroyed by bombing in November 1940. The competition for a new building, held in 1951, was won by Sir Basil Spence. The Queen laid the foundation stone of the new Coventry Cathedral in 1956 and in May 1962 signed its Sentence of Consecration. The vast tapestry of Christ in Glory, set behind the High Altar, was designed by Graham Sutherland. One of Sutherland's preliminary designs for the tapestry was acquired by The Duke of Edinburgh in July of the same year.

1963

In February–March 1963 The Queen paid her second visit to Australasia. On 18 February she opened the New Zealand Parliament in Wellington, wearing this beautiful ivory silk satin dress.

This greenstone mere (or club) was presented to The Queen by the Maori chief Paora Rerepu Te Urupu in 1964, the year after her visit to New Zealand. The chief's forebears had used the mere to fight Europeans; he hoped that it would now assist in the campaign to bring Europeans and Maoris closer together.

Prince Edward, The Queen's fourth child, was born at Buckingham Palace on 10 March 1964. Later that year the infant Prince was photographed by Cecil Beaton with his mother and Prince Andrew. He was christened in the Private Chapel at Windsor Castle on 2 May.

His richly decorated christening cake was crowned with a crib. Prince Edward's first public appearance came after the Trooping the Colour in the following month, when The Queen brought her baby son onto the palace balcony to show him to the crowds.

1965

In February 1965 The Queen and The Duke of Edinburgh paid a State Visit to Ethiopia at the invitation of Emperor Haile Selassie, who had himself paid a State Visit to the United Kingdom in October 1954. The Queen's dress of green silk celebrates one of the national colours of Ethiopia and was designed by Norman Hartnell for the State Banquet in Addis Ababa. The silver cross was given to The Queen by the Emperor in 1969.

The final of the 1966 World Cup was played at Wembley Stadium on 30 July. The Queen was clearly delighted to present the cup to Bobby Moore, the captain of the England team. The Queen's programme for this famous match was given a gilded leather cover, in keeping with the importance of the occasion.

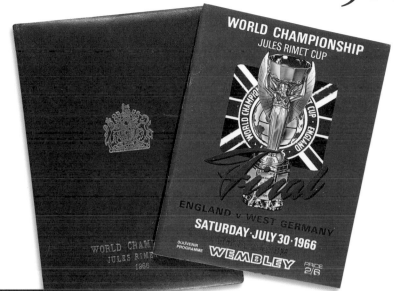

1967

Every year, usually in late October or early November, the Sovereign drives in state to the Palace of Westminster for the State Opening of Parliament. Each new session of Parliament opens with The Queen's Speech, delivered to the members of both Houses in the House of Lords. For the ceremony itself she wears the Imperial State Crown.

For the journeys between Buckingham Palace and the Palace of Westminster for the State Opening of Parliament, The Queen wears the magnificent Diamond Diadem, originally made for George IV in 1820.

1968

Some of the most memorable images of The Queen were taken by the photographer Cecil Beaton, who died in 1980. This photograph is from his last royal sitting, which took place at Buckingham Palace in October 1968. On that occasion Beaton took the unusual step of asking The Queen to wear her admiral's cloak – thus creating a dramatically stark image, quite different from his previous shots of The Queen.

In December 1968 The Queen opened the new Royal Mint in Llantrisant, Glamorganshire. The transfer of the Mint from London coincided with the start of work on the new decimal coinage, which was introduced in 1971.

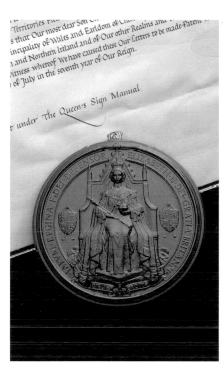

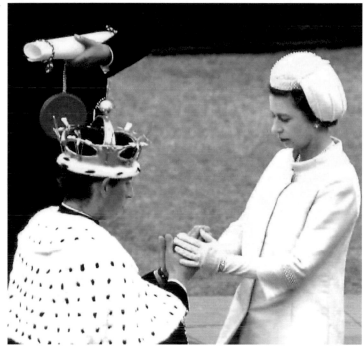

Prince Charles had been created Prince of Wales in July 1958, but it was not until July 1969 that The Queen formally invested him with this title, at Caernarvon Castle. Unusually, the Great Seal attached to the letters patent bearing the royal sign manual was made with blue (rather than red) wax. Most elements of the investiture were specially designed for the occasion by the Earl of Snowdon. The Prince's coronet was made by Louis Osman.

1970

The Queen's five-week visit to Australia, between late March and early May 1970, coincided with the bicentennial celebrations of Cook's first landing in Australia. For much of the visit the Royal Family was based on HMY *Britannia*, here shown being escorted into Brisbane harbour. The tour featured in The Queen's Christmas broadcast of 1970, filmed in her Sitting Room at Buckingham Palace.

Membership of the Order of the Thistle is the highest honour in Scotland. The Queen is Sovereign Head of the Order and personally appoints Knights Brethren of the Thistle. The Queen and Duke of Edinburgh are here shown at the start of their approach to St Giles' Cathedral, Edinburgh, for the Thistle service in July 1971. The diamond-set Thistle badge and star shown here were both once worn by Prince Albert. The badge was probably made for George IV.

1972

In February and March 1972 The Queen made an extensive tour of South-East Asia and the Indian Ocean. In mid-February she was the guest of King Bhumibol and Queen Sirikit of Thailand. The beaded yellow panels in The Queen's dress match the sash of the Order of Chakri, the Thai national order.

The Silver Wedding Anniversary of The Queen and The Duke of Edinburgh was marked by a Thanksgiving Service in Westminster Abbey, followed by a ceremonial drive to the City of London for lunch at Guildhall. When the royal landau reached the City boundary at Temple Bar, the Lord Mayor made his traditional gesture to the Sovereign by offering her his sword of state, point downwards. As custom dictates, after touching the sword The Queen continued on her way.

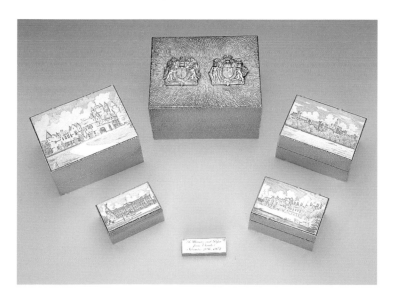

Among the many anniversary gifts to The Queen and Prince Philip was this nest of silver boxes with engraved views of the royal residences. It was commissioned by The Prince of Wales from the goldsmith Gerald Benney.

1973

One of the fixed points in The Queen's calendar is the Royal Maundy Service, on Maundy Thursday (the day before Good Friday). In 1973 the service was held at Westminster Abbey. The number of Maundy Money recipients corresponds to the Sovereign's age. All recipients are pensioners, nominated for their service to the Church and to the community. Each one receives a red bag containing £5.50 in cash, and a white bag containing silver Maundy coins of the same value in pence as The Queen's age.

OFFICE

FOR

THE ROYAL MAUNDY

WESTMINSTER ABBEY

MAUNDY THURSDAY

19 APRIL, 1973

In 1973 The Queen was in her forty-seventh year, so each of the 47 male and 47 female recipients were given 47 pence in Maundy Money, made up from newly minted four-coin sets of silver coinage.

Like the Queen Mother before her, The Queen is a keen admirer of, and participant in, 'the sport of kings'. Her particular interest, as owner and breeder, is flat racing. In 1974 her filly Highclere won both the One Thousand Guineas (below) and the Prix de Diane – the first filly ever to win both races. This painting shows the jockey Joe Mercer riding Highclere in 1974.

The royal racing colours – purple body with gold braid, scarlet sleeves and black velvet cap with gold tassel – were first registered in 1875 by the future King Edward VII.

1975

A significant stage of the transition from Empire to a Commonwealth of self-governing nations was reached in 1975 when – on the advice of ministers in the respective countries – The Queen instituted the Order of Australia (left) in February, followed by The Queen's Service Order, New Zealand (right), in March; twelve years later she also instituted the Order of New Zealand. In Canada a similar change had already been heralded by the introduction of the Order of Canada (centre) in 1967, and the Order of Military Merit in 1972. The Queen is Sovereign of each of these Orders.

Among the many gifts which The Queen received in her fiftieth birthday year in 1976 was this engraved glass vase and cover. It was presented by the Royal Company of Archers and shows archers in action, with bows and arrows. It served as the Archers' special royal gift or 'reddendo', to mark the tercentenary of their foundation in 1676, and was presented during The Queen's summer visit to Holyroodhouse. The Royal Company is the Sovereign's bodyguard in Scotland.

At the start of each of The Queen's annual visits to her official residence in Scotland, the Palace of Holyroodhouse, Her Majesty receives the ceremonial key to the Palace.

1977

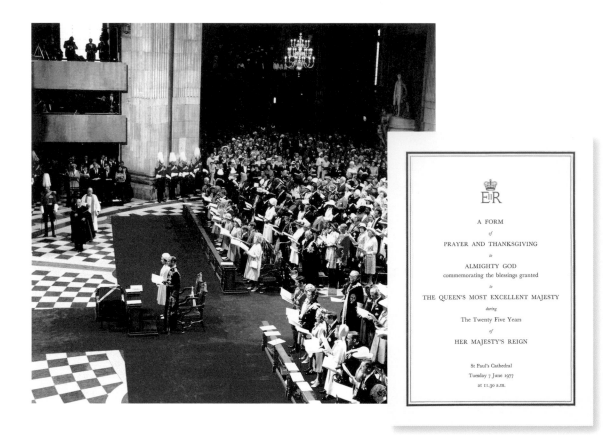

The twenty-fifth anniversary of The Queen's accession was celebrated in 1977. The high point of the Silver Jubilee year was the Service of Thanksgiving in St Paul's Cathedral on 7 June, followed by a luncheon at Guildhall. In Her Majesty's speech there, she recalled how 'when I was twenty-one I pledged my life to the service of our people and I asked for God's help to make good that vow', declaring that 'Although that vow was made in my salad days, when I was green in judgement, I do not retract one word of it.'

On 4 May at the Palace of Westminster both Houses of Parliament had presented loyal addresses to The Queen. This tiny book includes printed transcripts of The Queen's responses to these addresses – all with the keynote of national unity. It is shown here alongside a 25-pence piece issued to celebrate the Silver Jubilee.

The Queen's summer programme included six Jubilee tours in the United Kingdom and Northern Ireland, covering 36 counties. Here she is shown visiting Highbury Fields in north London.

Over the Jubilee weekend, street parties were held throughout the United Kingdom. Here families in Woodford Bridge, Essex, celebrate the Silver Jubilee.

1977

Britannia was used for two major Commonwealth tours in 1977: the first covered the Pacific Islands, New Zealand and Australia; the second covered Canada and the Caribbean. In the course of the year, The Queen travelled an estimated 56,000 miles.

The Naval Review at Spithead was one of the highlights of the Silver Jubilee year. The Queen, on board HMY *Britannia*, reviewed the fleet assembled in the Solent for the occasion.

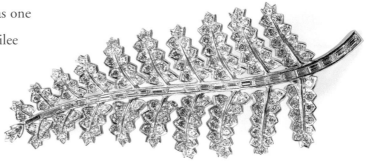

When visiting the Maori people at Gisborne, New Zealand, in February 1977, The Queen wore the Maori feather cloak that she had been given in Arawa Park, Rotorua, on her first Commonwealth Tour in 1953–4. The diamond and platinum fern brooch (above) had been a gift from the Women of Auckland on the same tour.

Mark Cornacka's marble group of five Inuit, dressed in traditional costume, was one of many Silver Jubilee gifts to The Queen during her visit to Canada.

This lapel button and gold medal were issued in Canada to commemorate the Silver Jubilee. The medal bears a maple leaf on the reverse.

1978

This photograph of The Queen's first grandchild, Peter Phillips, was released on 21 April 1978 to celebrate her fifty-second birthday. Peter Phillips is the elder of the two children of Princess Anne and her first husband, Captain Mark Phillips. The photograph was taken by The Queen's brother-in-law, the Earl of Snowdon.

In February and March 1979 The Queen paid
an official visit to the Middle East, including
two days in Qatar. During a visit to the
National Museum in Doha she was given
a studded brass box (right) containing rock
samples and inscribed with the following
words: *British Geologists were the first pioneers
in deciphering the occurrence of Petroleum
in the Strata of Qatar since the times of
Your Majesty's Great Ancestress Queen Victoria.*

This model dhow,
complete with the
national flag of Qatar,
was another gift on
the visit. Dhows were
a crucial part of the
region's sea-trading
activity during the
early history of the
nation.

1980

In August 1980 Queen Elizabeth The Queen
Mother celebrated her eightieth birthday.
This photograph of Queen Elizabeth with
her two daughters was taken by Norman
Parkinson to mark the occasion.

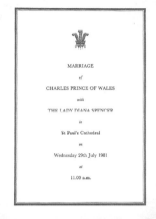

MARRIAGE
of
CHARLES PRINCE OF WALES
with
THE LADY DIANA SPENCER
in
St Paul's Cathedral
on
Wednesday 29th July 1981
at
11.00 a.m.

The marriage of The Prince of Wales and Lady
Diana Spencer took place at St Paul's Cathedral
on 29 July 1981. The Queen and The Princess
of Wales gathered with the bridesmaids in the
Picture Gallery at Buckingham Palace after
the ceremony. The little girl in front of
The Queen is Clementine Hambro, the great-
granddaughter of her first Prime Minister,
Winston Churchill. The photographer, the
Earl of Lichfield, was the grandson of
The Queen Mother's brother Jock, and thus
The Queen's first cousin once removed.

CEREMONIAL

The Marriage of
HIS ROYAL HIGHNESS
THE PRINCE OF WALES
with
THE LADY DIANA SPENCER
at
ST. PAUL'S CATHEDRAL
on
Wednesday 29th July, 1981
at 11.00 a.m.

1982

Prince William, the elder child of The Prince and Princess of Wales, was born on 21 June 1982 and was christened in the Music Room at Buckingham Palace on 4 August.

Queen Elizabeth The Queen Mother, whose eighty-second birthday this was, sits on the right in this family group.

The Order of Merit, founded by King Edward VII in 1902, is awarded by the Sovereign to those who have rendered exceptionally meritorious service. It is in the sole gift of the Sovereign. In a special ceremony at the Rashtrapati Bhavan in November 1983, Mother Teresa of Calcutta became an Honorary Member of the Order. At the time The Queen was attending a meeting of the Commonwealth Heads of Government in New Delhi.

1983

Balmoral Castle, Aberdeenshire, has been one of the Sovereign's private residences since the estate was acquired by Queen Victoria and Prince Albert in 1852. The Queen has visited Balmoral regularly since childhood, and now spends two months there every summer.

In 1983 she commissioned a series of photographs of the castle from Sir Geoffrey Shakerley, using the viewpoints that had been used for watercolours made for Queen Victoria.

The view of the Dee Valley and Invercauld from Ballochbuie Forest was painted by The Prince of Wales in 1988.

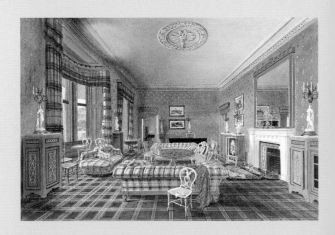

In late March 1984 The Queen and Duke
of Edinburgh paid a State Visit to Jordan,
as guests of King Hussein and Queen Noor.
The King had dispatched the formal
invitation leading to this visit in August 1983.

This mother-of-pearl casket, containing a late
nineteenth-century bridal necklace and
embroidered cloth, was given to The Queen
in Aqaba in the course of her visit. It was
made in Bethlehem.

1985

Each year the Sovereign's official birthday in June is marked by The Queen's Birthday Parade on Horse Guards, Whitehall. The Queen took the salute on horseback (riding side-saddle) from 1947 until 1986. Her mount from 1969 was Burmese (1962–90), a black mare bred and presented by the Royal Canadian Mounted Police. Following Burmese's retirement in 1986, The Queen has been driven the short distance between Buckingham Palace and Horse Guards in the Ivory Phaeton.

The Queen's side-saddle and Burmese's head-collar are both kept at Windsor. The head-collar also gives the names of Burmese's sire and dam.

The Queen personally takes the salute as the Colour is 'trooped' before her. The Guards regiments take turns to troop their Colour. In 1978 (below) it was the turn of the Grenadier Guards.

The colour of the plume in The Queen's hat changes according to the regiment whose colour is being trooped. In 1985 (see left and below) a red plume was worn for the trooping of the Coldstream Guards' Colour.

1986

Prince Andrew's photograph of The Queen was released in April 1986 to mark her sixtieth birthday. It was taken at Sandringham House, Norfolk, the private royal residence purchased for the future King Edward VII in 1862.

A vignette of The Queen on horseback in front of Sandringham House was included by Graham Rust in this bookplate design, a sixtieth birthday present from her first cousin Princess Alexandra, and the Princess's husband The Hon. Angus Ogilvy.

1986

In October 1986 The Queen and Duke of Edinburgh paid their first State Visit to China, as guests of President Li Xiannian. As well as being photographed among the terracotta warriors at Xian, The Queen herself photographed the Duke – for her own photograph album.

1987

Elizabeth R

Elizabeth the Second by the Grace of God OF THE UNITED KINGDOM OF GREAT BRITAIN AND NORTHERN IRELAND AND OF OUR OTHER REALMS AND TERRITORIES QUEEN HEAD OF THE COMMONWEALTH DEFENDER OF THE FAITH To Our Right Trusty and Right Entirely Beloved Cousin Miles Francis Stapleton, Duke of Norfolk, Knight of Our Most Noble Order of the Garter, Knight Grand Cross of Our Royal Victorian Order, Companion of Our Most Honourable Order of the Bath, Commander of Our Most Excellent Order of the British Empire, upon whom has been conferred the Decoration of the Military Cross, Earl Marshal and Our Hereditary Marshal of England: Greeting! WHEREAS We are desirous of defining and fixing the style by which Our Most Dear Daughter Her Royal Highness Princess Anne Elizabeth Alice Louise (Mrs Mark Phillips), Dame Grand Cross of Our Royal Victorian Order, shall be designated, We are pleased to declare that She shall henceforth be styled, Her Royal Highness The Princess Royal & Our Will and Pleasure therefore is that you, Our said Earl Marshal, to whom the cognizance of matters of this nature doth properly belong, do see this Our Order kept and that the same be duly registered in Our College of Arms to the end that Our Officers of Arms and all others upon occasion may take full notice & have knowledge thereof IN WITNESS whereof We have caused The Great Seal to be affixed to these Presents GIVEN at Our Court at Saint James's the Ninth day of June One Thousand Nine Hundred and Eighty-Seven, in the thirty-sixth year of Our Reign

BY THE QUEEN OF THE UNITED KINGDOM OF GREAT BRITAIN AND NORTHERN IRELAND AND OF HER OTHER REALMS AND TERRITORIES Signed with Her Own Hand

In June 1987 The Queen bestowed the title of Princess Royal on her only daughter, Princess Anne. The Princess had begun to undertake public engagements at the age of 18. In 1970 she was appointed President of the Save the Children Fund, in which she has been particularly active. The Princess Royal is also well known internationally as an Olympic-class horsewoman. She is a British representative on the International Olympic Committee and took part in London's successful bid to host the 2012 Olympic Games.

Each year The Queen and Duke of Edinburgh send about 750 Christmas cards, normally including a photograph from the past year on the cover. In 1988 the card (in the centre here) incorporated the Duchess of York's photograph of three generations of the Royal Family at Balmoral: The Queen holds the infant Princess Beatrice of York, born on 8 August, while Queen Elizabeth stands behind. The other cards shown here were sent between 1985 and 2002.

Sir Hugh Casson included this festive scene in a letter to The Queen.

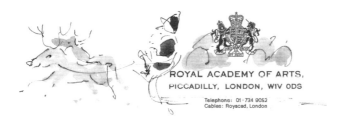

ROYAL ACADEMY OF ARTS,
PICCADILLY, LONDON, W1V 0DS

Telephone: 01-734 9052
Cables: Royacad, London

1989

The extraordinary events of 1989 included the April visit of President Gorbachev of the USSR to Windsor Castle as The Queen's guest. In early November of the same year the wall dividing East and West Berlin was demolished and – like many Western heads of state – The Queen was sent a portion of the demolished wall by the People of Germany. The Cold War was at an end.

WINDSOR CASTLE

Friday, 7th April, 1989
at 1.00 p.m.

The Chairman of the
Presidium of the Supreme
Soviet of the USSR and
Mrs. Gorbachev have been
invited to lunch.

From: The Deputy Private Secretary
28th March, 1989.

1990

The Queen's first visit to Iceland took place in late June 1990, when she was the guest of President Vigdis Finbogadottir. On the last day she was photographed walking through the evil-smelling hot sulphur springs at Krisuvik.

STATE VISIT
TO ICELAND

OF
HER MAJESTY
QUEEN ELIZABETH II
AND
HIS ROYAL HIGHNESS
THE PRINCE PHILIP,
DUKE OF EDINBURGH

25–27 JUNE 1990

Wednesday, 27 June

10:13 a.m.	Departure by car (5 kms)
10:25 a.m.	Arrival at Fossvogur Cemetery
	Wreath-laying Ceremony at Commonwealth War Graves in the presence of Veterans and the British Community
10:45 a.m.	Departure by car for Bessastaðir
	A moment of prayer in the Church
	Continue to Krisuvík Geothermal Area
12:45 p.m.	Arrival at Keflavík International Airport
12:55 p.m.	His Royal Highness The Prince Philip, Duke of Edinburgh, departs in an aircraft of the Queen's Flight for the United Kingdom
1:00 p.m.	Her Majesty Queen Elizabeth II departs in a Canadian Forces Aircraft for Canada

1991

In May 1991 The Queen revisited the United States, as the guest of President George Bush. Her programme included a formal address to a meeting of both Houses of Congress. In the course of the visit she received this engraved glass flower bowl, decorated with references to flowers in Shakespeare's works.

THE STATE VISIT
TO WASHINGTON, D.C.
OF
HER MAJESTY QUEEN ELIZABETH II
OF
THE UNITED KINGDOM
OF
GREAT BRITAIN AND NORTHERN IRELAND
AND
HIS ROYAL HIGHNESS THE PRINCE PHILIP
DUKE OF EDINBURGH

MAY 14 TO 17, 1991

THURSDAY
MAY 16, 1991 (Continued)   WASHINGTON, D.C.

11:25 am   Mr. Russ, Ms. Pope, and the
            Congressional Escort Committee escort
            The Queen and The Duke of Edinburgh to
            the Great Hall of the United States
            House of Representatives via the Center
            Door.

11:29 am   The Queen, accompanied by The Duke of
            Edinburgh, is announced by Mr. James
            Malloy, Doorkeeper of the United States
            House of Representatives, to The
            Honorable Thomas S. Foley, Speaker of
            the United States House of
            Representatives.

11:30 am   Address by Her Majesty Queen Elizabeth
            II of the United Kingdom of Great
            Britain and Northern Ireland before a
            Joint Meeting of the United States
            Congress in the Great Hall of the
            United States House of Representatives
            at the United States Capitol.

            At the conclusion of the Address, The
            Queen, accompanied by The Duke of
            Edinburgh, is escorted to the Speaker's
            Room, H-204, by Mr. Russ and Ms. Pope.

                                                -75-

The year 1992 was one of mixed fortunes.
It began with the fortieth anniversary of
The Queen's accession, on 6 February,
which was marked by Ted Hughes
with his poem 'The Unicorn'.

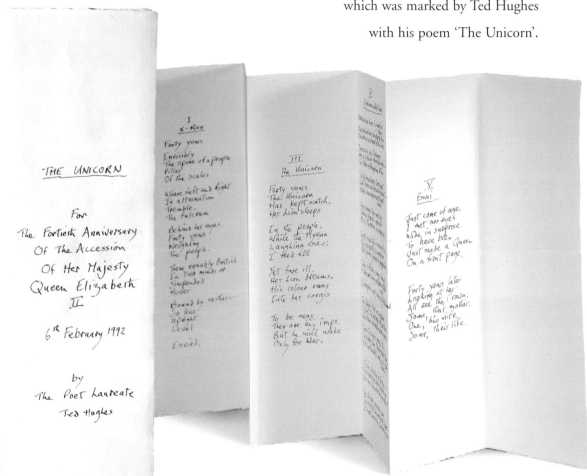

THE UNICORN

For
The Fortieth Anniversary
Of The Accession
Of Her Majesty
Queen Elizabeth
II

6th February 1992

by
The Poet Laureate
Ted Hughes

I
X-Ray

Forty years

Invisibly
The spine of a people
Pillar
Of the scales

Where left and Right
In alternation
Tremble.
The fulcrum

Behind her eyes.
Forty years
Weighing
The people.

These equally British
In Two minds or
Suspended
Hover

Bound by neither
To live/
Upright
Level

Envied.

III
The Unicorn

Forty years
The Unicorn
Has kept watch.
Her Lion sleeps

In the people.
While the Hyena
Laughing cries:
I feed all

Yet fare ill.
Her Lion Beams.
His colour runs
Into her corgis

To be near.
They are his imps.
But he will wake
Only for War.

V
Envoi

Just come of age
I met her eyes
Wide in surprise
To have been
Just made a Queen
On a front page.

Forty years later
Laughing at her
All see the Crown.
Some, their mother.
One, his wife.
Some, their life.

99

1992

On 20 November – The Queen's forty-fifth wedding anniversary – a major fire broke out at Windsor Castle. Parts of both the State and the Private Apartments were destroyed, but over the next five years a major restoration programme was completed. In the new Private Chapel the stained-glass window, designed by The Duke of Edinburgh, records the fire-fighting and salvage operation.

To fund the restoration work on Windsor Castle, The Queen decided to open Buckingham Palace to the public for the first time. In the space of eight weeks, a total of nearly 380,000 people came to the Palace and the queue stretched back down the Mall. A substantial further sum was raised through the sale of souvenirs, produced by the Royal Collection.

In 1993 The Queen and Prince Philip visited Hungary as the guests of President Arpad Goncz. This was their first State Visit to a country in the former Eastern Bloc.

1994

The Channel Tunnel was officially opened
by The Queen and President Mitterand of
France in May 1994, after many years of
discussion and engineering work. A fragment
of the inaugural ribbon cut by Queen and
President was kept as a souvenir, together
with the gilt commemorative medal.

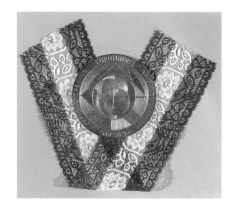

The fiftieth anniversary of VE Day, which
marked the end of the Second World War
in Europe, was celebrated in May 1995.
The same three royal ladies had been
photographed in the same location
– the balcony at Buckingham Palace –
fifty years before.

1996

The visit of Nelson Mandela, President of South Africa, to London in July 1996 marked an important point in the relationship between the two nations. The Queen was photographed standing beside the President before the State Banquet held at Buckingham Palace in his honour. In the previous year President Mandela had welcomed The Queen and Prince Philip to South Africa.

STATE BANQUET
IN HONOUR OF

THE PRESIDENT
OF THE
REPUBLIC OF SOUTH AFRICA

BUCKINGHAM PALACE
TUESDAY, 9th JULY, 1996

Among the gifts that President Mandela brought to London was this silk headscarf, decorated with animals and hunters.

The tragic death of Diana, Princess of Wales,
at the end of August 1997 led to a national
outpouring of grief. On the day before the
Princess's funeral The Queen and Duke of
Edinburgh viewed the tributes left outside
the gates of Buckingham Palace.

1997

In November a Thanksgiving
Service was held at Westminster
Abbey to celebrate the Golden
Wedding Anniversary of
The Queen and Duke
of Edinburgh.

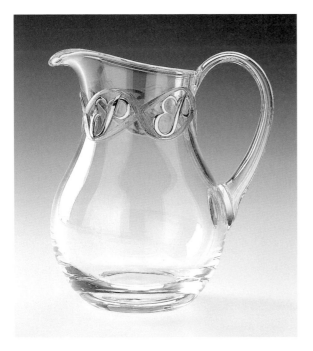

Princess Margaret's wedding anniversary
present to her sister and brother-in-law was
a glass jug with the initials E and P
overlaid in gold around the neck.

In the following year The Prince of Wales celebrated his fiftieth birthday. On the eve of his birthday The Queen gave a party at Buckingham Palace to celebrate The Prince's public work. Among the guests were many associated with his charities. The Queen made a congratulatory speech in the course of the evening, to which The Prince responded.

RECEPTION
FOR
THE PRINCE OF WALES
BUCKINGHAM PALACE

FRIDAY, 13TH NOVEMBER, 1998

1999

The end of the second millennium was marked by a reception, attended by The Queen and her Prime Minister Tony Blair, in the new Millennium Dome at Greenwich. The Queen had been shown a model of the dome during her visit to the Royal Institution of Chartered Surveyors in July 1999.

On a barge in the River Thames at Greenwich, The Queen lit the flame that fired the National Millennium Beacon, the first in a string of 10,000 beacons to be lit across the nation.

In August, Queen Elizabeth The Queen
Mother celebrated her hundredth birthday.
The Queen's personalised telegram was
delivered to Clarence House before the Royal
Family gathered at Buckingham Palace for
lunch and the traditional balcony appearance.

On your 100th Birthday all the family join with me in sending you our loving best wishes for this special day

Lilibet

BUCKINGHAM PALACE
LONDON SW1A 1AA

ROYAL MAIL

Her Majesty Queen Elizabeth The Queen Mother
Clarence House
St. James's
London
SW1A 1BA

2000

The Queen and Duke of Edinburgh were received in audience by Pope John Paul II during their visit to the Vatican in October 2000. The Queen's gift to the Pope was a set of facsimiles of Canaletto drawings in the Royal Collection. The white leather box containing the facsimiles was specially bound for the occasion in the Royal Bindery at Windsor, and stamped with the official crowned EIIR tool.

The annual Remembrance Sunday Service
at the Cenotaph, Whitehall, each November
is a key event in the royal calendar. On this
occasion the whole nation, led by the
Sovereign, pays homage to those who have
died in the service of their country.
The Queen has attended the service from
her earliest years. She is here shown in
contemplation during the two-minute silence
at the service in 2001, shortly before laying
her wreath.

2002

The Golden Jubilee year opened with the deaths of two of The Queen's closest relations – first Princess Margaret, in February; and then Queen Elizabeth, in late March. Before The Queen Mother's funeral in Westminster Abbey, her coffin lay in state in Westminster Hall. This watercolour, commissioned by The Queen, shows the catafalque guarded by Queen Elizabeth's four grandsons.

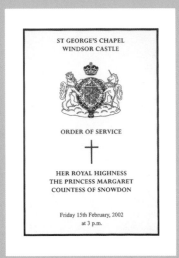

ST GEORGE'S CHAPEL
WINDSOR CASTLE

ORDER OF SERVICE

✝

HER ROYAL HIGHNESS
THE PRINCESS MARGARET
COUNTESS OF SNOWDON

Friday 15th February, 2002
at 3 p.m.

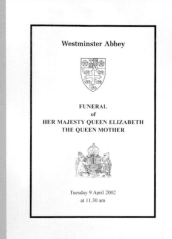

Westminster Abbey

FUNERAL
of
HER MAJESTY QUEEN ELIZABETH
THE QUEEN MOTHER

Tuesday 9 April 2002
at 11.30 am

For the remainder of the Jubilee year, The Queen resumed her round of public duties. In this photograph she wears the Family Orders of King George VI and King George V, with Garter Star and sash, and the Grand Duchess Vladimir's tiara, set with pearls.

2002

The Golden Jubilee culminated in a series of events in London in early June. The Prom at the Palace (featuring classical music) on 1 June was the first public concert ever to be staged in the grounds of Buckingham Palace.

Two days later the same stage was used for the Party at the Palace, which opened to the sound of the national anthem, played by Brian May (guitarist of the rock band Queen) on the roof of the Palace. After the concert The Queen joined the performers – including Paul McCartney, Cliff Richard and Andrea Corr – on the stage.

Following their return, The Queen and Prince Philip appeared on the Palace balcony, and admired a flypast including Concorde.

On the following day, 4 June, The Queen travelled in the Gold State Coach from Buckingham Palace to St Paul's Cathedral for a Service of Thanksgiving. The coach, made for George III in 1762, was also used by The Queen at the time of her coronation in 1953, and for the Silver Jubilee in 1977.

2002

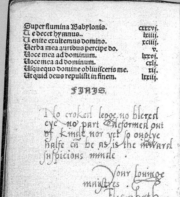

The Golden Jubilee year was also marked by the opening of two new Queen's Galleries, in London and Edinburgh. The Prince of Wales, Chairman of the Royal Collection Trustees, greeted The Queen prior to the opening of the new Queen's Gallery at Buckingham Palace in May. The first exhibition, *Royal Treasures*, included many of the additions made to the Royal Collection during The Queen's reign, some of which are shown opposite. These included the portrait of The Queen painted by Lucian Freud.

2003

Prince William celebrated his twenty-first birthday in June 2003, and appeared with The Queen on the balcony of Buckingham Palace to watch the flypast after the Trooping the Colour ceremony in the same month.

This photograph, taken by The Duke of Edinburgh, shows Philip Jackson's equestrian figure of The Queen, which was unveiled in Windsor Great Park in 2003. It was the Golden Jubilee gift to the Sovereign from the Crown Estate.

The Queen has been an active horsewoman throughout her life. This photograph was taken at Windsor on 10 April 2004. The Queen rides Tinkerbell, while her granddaughter Zara Phillips (on the left) rides Tiger Lily, Tinkerbell's daughter, and The Princess Royal (on the right) rides Peter Pan, Tinkerbell's son. Forty years earlier, The Queen was recorded riding along the racecourse at Ascot.

2005

In February 2005 The Queen hosted a dinner for the International Olympic Committee's evaluation commission at Buckingham Palace. London's bid for the Olympics was successful and the 2012 Games will be held in the nation's capital city.

The Prince of Wales's marriage to Camilla Parker Bowles in April 2005 was an event of particular happiness for the Royal Family. The Queen is shown with The Prince of Wales and The Duchess of Cornwall at the reception in St George's Hall following the marriage and Thanksgiving Service. Slices of wedding cake were distributed in decorated tin boxes.

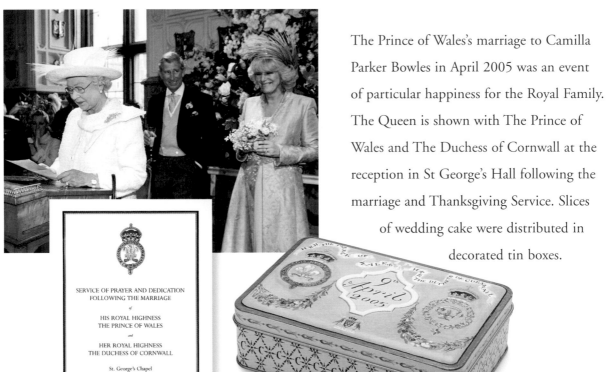

SERVICE OF PRAYER AND DEDICATION
FOLLOWING THE MARRIAGE
of
HIS ROYAL HIGHNESS
THE PRINCE OF WALES
and
HER ROYAL HIGHNESS
THE DUCHESS OF CORNWALL

St. George's Chapel
Windsor Castle

Saturday, 9th April, 2005
2.30 p.m.

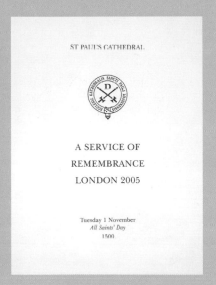

ST PAUL'S CATHEDRAL

A SERVICE OF
REMEMBRANCE
LONDON 2005

Tuesday 1 November
All Saints' Day
1500

After the London bombings in
July 2005, The Queen shared in
the national grief and mourning.
She was present at the Memorial
Service at St Paul's on All Saints'
Day, 1 November.

In October 2005 The Queen attended
the eightieth birthday celebrations of
Margaret Thatcher, her former
Prime Minister in London.

In the following month
Her Majesty visited RAF
Coltishall in Norfolk,
and witnessed a flypast of RAF
Jaguars in perfect formation.

2006

The Queen celebrated her eightieth birthday at Windsor in April 2006, followed by national celebrations in London in June.
In the course of 2006, Her Majesty received around 30,000 birthday cards, many of them specially made for the occasion.

The surviving members of SRS Duke of York, the Sea Rangers who had trained with Princess Elizabeth at Windsor in the 1940s, sent this charming card (far left).

Another card recorded The Queen's different residences and interests.

This eightieth birthday portrait was taken by
Jane Bown, born one year before The Queen.
It is one of sixty photographs of Her Majesty
exhibited at Windsor Castle in the Diamond
Jubilee year.

2006

At the end of June The Queen invited children and their parents to a special Children's Garden Party at Buckingham Palace. Guests were entertained by writers and storytellers, as well as by figures from the world of children's television – such as Postman Pat.

On June 15 there was a National Service of Thanksgiving at St Paul's Cathedral, followed by luncheon at Guildhall given by the Lord Mayor and the Corporation of London.

Children's
PARTY AT THE PALACE

The Queen and Prince Philip celebrated their Diamond Wedding Anniversary in November 2007. The Prince of Wales invited his parents to a family dinner at Clarence House, their first married home and now the home of The Prince of Wales and The Duchess of Cornwall.

At a Service of Thanksgiving in Westminster Abbey, The Queen greeted other couples who were celebrating their Diamond Wedding Anniversary in the same year.

A SERVICE OF CELEBRATION TO MARK
THE DIAMOND WEDDING ANNIVERSARY
OF
HER MAJESTY THE QUEEN
AND
HIS ROYAL HIGHNESS
THE DUKE OF EDINBURGH

Westminster Abbey

Monday 19 November 2007
11.30 a.m.

2007

In November 2007 The Queen led the meeting of the Commonwealth Heads of Government, held in Kampala.

Among the many gifts that she received on that occasion were a glass bottle containing water from the River Nile, a gold and diamond brooch in the shape of a spray of sorghum (a type of millet; from the President of Botswana), and a black ceramic vase decorated with lizards (from the Prime Minister of Papua New Guinea).

On 26 March 2008 The Queen welcomed the President of France and Madame Sarkozy to Windsor Castle, at the start of their State Visit. For the State Banquet in St George's Hall, The Queen wore the magnificent ruby and diamond tiara made for her in 1973.

2008

Two months later, on 17 May, The Queen's eldest grandson, Peter Phillips, married Autumn Kelly at St George's Chapel, Windsor Castle. The wedding reception was held at Frogmore House in the Home Park. In this group photograph, the groom's mother (The Princess Royal) and father (Captain Mark Phillips) stand behind The Queen and Prince Philip. Members of the bride's family are on the right of the photograph.

Frogmore has been used as a royal retreat, as well as for entertaining, since the late eighteenth century, when it was acquired for George III's wife Queen Charlotte. In this photograph The Queen is shown in the garden of Frogmore House with her husband and young family – including The Princess Royal on the left – in 1965.

In 2009 the Commonwealth celebrated its sixtieth anniversary. Each year Commonwealth Day is marked on the second Monday of March. The Commonwealth Mace (above), presented to The Queen in 1992, is carried in procession during the Commonwealth Day Service – a colourful inter-faith occasion at Westminster Abbey.

In November 2009 the Commonwealth Heads of Government meeting was held in Trinidad and Tobago. During The Queen's visit to Trinidad, she met local children dressed in carnival costume, and received a signed cricket bat from Brian Lara.

2009

The first awards were presented at Catterick in August 2009. In the following month The Queen herself visited Catterick, and made a number of personal presentations of the Elizabeth Cross.

In 2009 The Queen introduced a new award – the Elizabeth Cross – to provide national recognition for the families of Armed Forces personnel who have died on operations or as a result of an act of terrorism. The arms of the cross bear floral symbols representing England (a rose), Scotland (a thistle), Ireland (a shamrock) and Wales (a daffodil).

On 28 June 2010 The Queen arrived in
Canada at the start of an eight-day visit
which coincided with the annual Canada Day
celebrations. On that occasion The Queen
wore the platinum and diamond maple-leaf
brooch that had been given by her father
to her mother in 1939, just before their
State Visit to Canada. The maple leaf
is the national symbol
of Canada.

2010

On 6 July 2010 The Queen addressed the
United Nations in New York – over fifty years
after her first UN address. She appealed to all
countries to work together as hard as ever –
and to truly be united nations.

The aquamarine and diamond
clips that she wore on this
occasion had been an
eighteenth birthday present
from the King and Queen
in 1944.

The Royal Family gathered in London in April 2011 for the wedding of The Prince of Wales's eldest son, Prince William (created The Duke of Cambridge shortly before), to Catherine Middleton. After the marriage ceremony in Westminster Abbey, a reception was held in Buckingham Palace.

The bride's veil was held in place by a diamond tiara lent by The Queen. The tiara had been given by King George VI to Queen Elizabeth in 1936 and the Queen presented it to her daughter in 1944, for her eighteenth birthday.

2011

In May 2011 The Queen visited the Republic of Ireland for the first time, heralding a new era in relations between the United Kingdom and Ireland. In her speech at the State Banquet in Dublin Castle, Her Majesty declared: 'We celebrate together the widespread spirit of goodwill and deep mutual understanding that has served to make the relationship more harmonious, close as good neighbours should always be.'

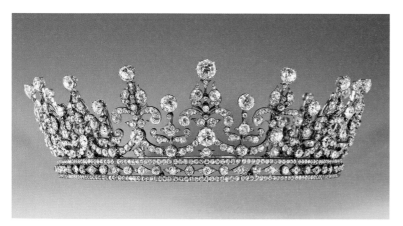

For the Banquet The Queen wore the diamond tiara given to the future Queen Mary as a wedding present from 'the Girls of Great Britain and Ireland' in 1893. In 1947 Queen Mary had given the tiara to her grand-daughter, Princess Elizabeth, as a wedding present.

In early February 2012 The Queen will reach the sixtieth anniversary of her accession. The Diamond Jubilee celebrations will be concentrated in early June, but will extend throughout the year – coinciding with the London Olympics.

The Diamond Jubilee weekend in early June will see a national celebration of The Queen's 60-year reign, with events including a Thames River Pageant, a Service of Thanksgiving at St Paul's Cathedral and a carriage procession through the streets to Buckingham Palace.

Similar events were included in the programme of celebrations for Queen Victoria's Diamond Jubilee over 100 years ago, underlining the strength and longevity of the traditions surrounding the British Monarchy. **"God Save The Queen!"**

ILLUSTRATIONS

Unless otherwise stated, all illustrations are The Royal Collection © 2011, HM Queen Elizabeth II. Items with RA references are The Royal Archives © 2011, HM Queen Elizabeth II. Royal Collection Publications are grateful for permission to reproduce those items listed below for which copyright is not held by the Royal Collection or Royal Archives.

Page 2
• *The Queen returns to Buckingham Palace after the Coronation, 2 June 1953,* photograph © UPPA/Photoshot

Page 3
• Coronation Stole, 1953, cloth of gold (RCIN 31795; detail). Crown © The Royal Collection
• *The Queen in Coronation Robes, 1953,* photograph by Cecil Beaton (RCIN 2507923; detail)
• *The Queen at the State Opening of Parliament, 13 November 2002,* photograph: PA

Page 4
• *Queen Victoria: Diamond Jubilee portrait, July 1893,* photograph by W. & D. Downey (RCIN 2912658)
• Queen Victoria's small diamond crown, 1870, Garrard, diamonds and silver (RCIN 31705)

Page 5
• Cup and saucer, 1926, Paragon China Ltd., Longton, Staffordshire, bone china (RCIN 54801.a-b)
• *King George VI and Queen Elizabeth with Princesses Elizabeth and Margaret, 15 December 1936,* photograph by Marcus Adams (RCIN 2999914)
• Double-frame containing two photographs from Princess Elizabeth's first sitting with Marcus Adams, 2 December 1926, leather with gelatin silver prints (RCIN 2943742)

Page 6
• *No. 17 Bruton Street, London W1* (RCIN 2002127). Copyright Reserved/The Royal Collection
• *Princess Elizabeth, May 1926,* photograph Speaight Ltd. (RCIN 2999931). Copyright Reserved/The Royal Collection
• *The Duke of York and Princess Elizabeth, 2 December 1926,* photograph by Marcus Adams (RCIN 2999845)

Page 7
• *Group photograph at Buckingham Palace following the Christening of Princess Elizabeth, 29 May 1926* (RCIN 2999930)
• Princess Elizabeth's christening cup, Henry Hodson Plante, silver, presented 1926 (RCIN 50931)

Page 8
• *Princess Elizabeth with the Countess of Strathmore, 1927,* photograph by Frederick and Hubert Thurston (RCIN 2999917). Copyright Reserved/The Royal Collection
• *Princess Elizabeth in a high chair, May 1927,* photograph by Frederick and Hubert Thurston (RCIN 2999927). Copyright Reserved/The Royal Collection
• *Princess Elizabeth on a window ledge, May 1927,* photograph by Frederick and Hubert Thurston (RCIN 2999928). Copyright Reserved/The Royal Collection

Page 9
• *Princess Elizabeth pushing a dolls' pram in Piccadilly, 1928,* photograph by Jack Esten, Camera Press
• *Princess Elizabeth with her chin in her hands, 5 July 1928,* photograph by Marcus Adams (RCIN 2585300)
• Doll, *c.*1910, Simon & Halbig/Kammer & Reinhart, biscuit porcelain with cream silk dress (RCIN 64204)

Page 10
• *Princess Elizabeth with lilies, 1929,* photograph by The Duke of York, later King George VI (RCIN 2999926)

Page 11
• *Princess Elizabeth with umbrella, 1928,* photograph by The Duke of York, later King George VI (RCIN 2999820; detail)

Page12
• *Princess Elizabeth with Queen Mary at the Naval and Military Tournament, 29 May 1930* (RCIN 2999842). Copyright Reserved/The Royal Collection
• *Princess Elizabeth in an open carriage outside No. 145 Piccadilly, c.1930* (RCIN 2999841). Copyright Reserved/The Royal Collection

Page 13
• 'Lilibet's first letter' to Queen Mary, April 1931 (RA GV/CC 14/63)
• *Princess Elizabeth on her tricycle, 1931* (RCIN 2002135). Copyright Reserved/The Royal Collection
• *Princess Elizabeth and the Countess of Airlie, Glamis, 1931* (RCIN 2999840). Copyright Reserved/The Royal Collection

Page 14
• *Princesses Elizabeth and Margaret on a rocking horse at St Paul's Walden Bury, August 1932,* photograph by Frederick Thurston (RCIN 2999918). Copyright Reserved/The Royal Collection
• *Princess Elizabeth on her Shetland pony, c.1932* (RCIN 2999839). Copyright Reserved/The Royal Collection

Page 15
• Philip de László, *Princess Elizabeth, 1933,* oil on canvas (RCIN 409002)

Page 16
• *King George V and Queen Mary with the Duchess of York and Princesses Elizabeth and Margaret outside Y Bwthyn Bach, May 1933,* photograph by Princess Victoria (RCIN 2999838)

Page 17
• Letter from Princess Elizabeth to Queen Mary, 16 February 1934 (RA GV/CC 14/65)
• *Princess Elizabeth as a bridesmaid at the wedding of the Duke and Duchess of Kent, 29 November 1934,* photograph by Bassano (RCIN 2999837)

Page 30
• *Princess Elizabeth engaged in vehicle maintenance duties as a member of the ATS, April 1945,* photograph by IWM (RCIN 2002230). Camera Press
• Princess Elizabeth's ATS uniform, photograph by Joe Little
• Detail of name tape in Princess Elizabeth's ATS uniform, photograph: copyright Newsteam.co.uk

Page 31
• *Princess Elizabeth launches Britain's giant new aircraft carrier, HMS Eagle, at Harland and Wolff shipyard, Belfast, 19 March 1946* (RCIN 2002266). Copyright Reserved/The Royal Collection
• *Princess Elizabeth, wearing the robe of an Ovate, received into the order of Druids by the Arch-Druid, at the National Eisteddfod of Wales, Mountain Ash, 6 August 1946* (RCIN 2002291). Copyright Reserved/The Royal Collection

Page 32
• The Queen's 'South Africa' diamond necklace, 1947, Garrard (RCIN 200152)
• *Princesses Elizabeth and Margaret on HMS Vanguard with the ship's cat during the Royal Tour of South Africa, 1947* (RCIN 2999831). Copyright Reserved/The Royal Collection
• *Princesses Margaret and Elizabeth on the footplate of one of the engines hauling the Royal Train, with the South African Minister of Transport (Hon. F.C. Sturrock), in South Africa, March 1947* (RCIN 2002312). Popperfoto.com/Getty Images

Page 33
• John Masefield, 'On the coming marriage of Her Royal Highness, The Princess Elizabeth', 1947, calligrapher Dorothy Hutton (RCIN 1047157). Copyright Reserved/The Royal Collection; reproduced with the permission of the Society of Authors as the Literary Representatives of the Estate of John Masefield
• The Queen's 'South Africa' diamond bracelet, 1947, Garrard (RCIN 200153)
• Princess Elizabeth's diamond engagement ring, 1947, Philip Antrobus Ltd. (RCIN 200165)

Page 34
• Princess Elizabeth's wedding dress, 1947, Norman Hartnell, duchesse satin, seed pearls, silver thread, appliqué tulle embroidery (RCIN 100019)
• Queen Mary's diamond fringe tiara, 1919, E. Wolff & Co. for Garrard (RCIN 200184)
• Diamond and pearl earrings, second quarter nineteenth century (RCIN 200187.1-2)

Page 35
• *Princess Elizabeth and The Duke of Edinburgh leaving Westminster Abbey following their marriage, 20 November 1947* (RCIN 2002399). TPS, Camera Press
• Order of Service for the Marriage Ceremony of Princess Elizabeth and Lieutenant Philip Mountbatten, 20 November 1947 (RA F&V/Weddings/1947/QEII)
• The Marriage Register for Westminster Abbey © Dean and Chapter of Westminster
• Quill pen used to sign the Marriage Register in 1947, gold (RCIN 48542)

Page 36
• Queen Mary's invitation, and Menu for the wedding breakfast at Buckingham Palace, 20 November 1947 (RA F&V/Weddings/1947/QEII)
• Wedding cake decoration in the form of a shoe, 1947, plastic with silver coating (RCIN 54844)
• *The royal wedding cakes, 20 November 1947* (RCIN 2940515). Copyright Reserved/The Royal Collection
• *Princess Elizabeth and The Duke of Edinburgh on their honeymoon,* November 1947 (RCIN 2584776). PA
• *Diamond Wedding Anniversary photograph of The Queen and The Duke of Edinburgh, November 2007,* photograph by Tim Graham (RCIN 2937789). Getty Images

Page 37
• Announcement of the birth of Prince Charles, 14 November 1948 (RA PS/GVI/PS 09091/6)
• Flower basket brooch, ?1920s, ?Cartier, rubies, emeralds, diamonds, sapphires (RCIN 200140)
• *Princess Elizabeth with the infant Prince Charles, 14 December 1948,* photograph by Cecil Beaton (RCIN 2999884)

Page 38
• *The Duke of Edinburgh and Princess Elizabeth on the roof of the Villa Guardamangia, Malta, 1949* (RCIN 2706274). Copyright Reserved/The Royal Collection
• Crocheted cotton mat, presented 1949 (RCIN 94724)

Page 39
• Silver figure of St George and the Dragon, designed by Edward Seago, c.1948 (RCIN 200163)
• *Rolls-Royce Phantom IV, coachwork by H.J. Mulliner & Co. Ltd., 1948* (RCIN 2002547). Copyright Reserved/The Royal Collection

Page 40
• *The Duke of Edinburgh with Princess Elizabeth, Prince Charles and the infant Princess Anne, 1950,* photograph by Baron Studios (RCIN 2999830)

Page 41
• *The Duke of Edinburgh and Princess Elizabeth, at the Royal 'Barn Dance', Rideau Hall, Ottawa, October 1951,* photographs by Frank Royal (RCIN 2003262, 2003264). Copyright 1951 National Film Board of Canada. All rights reserved.
• Evening gown, 1950s, Norman Hartnell, velvet and silk (RCIN 100037)

Page 42
• *The Queen arriving at London Airport from Kenya, 9 February 1952* (RCIN 2999978). Copyright Reserved/The Royal Collection
• The Williamson diamond brooch, 1952, Cartier (RCIN 200146)

Page 43
• Edward Halliday, *Maundy Thursday,* 1952, oil on canvas (RCIN 404800). Copyright Reserved/The Royal Collection
• Bracelet, 1952, Boucheron to a design by The Duke of Edinburgh, gold, platinum, sapphires, diamonds and rubies (RCIN 200151)
• *The Queen at Sandringham making her first Christmas broadcast, 25 December 1952* (RCIN 2004814). PA

Page 44
• Norman Hartnell, *Design for The Queen's Coronation Robe,* 1953, watercolour and bodycolour over pencil (RCIN 451858)
• *Miss R. Essam of the Royal School of Needlework embroidering The Queen's Coronation robe, 11 February 1953* (RCIN 2002692). Copyright Reserved/The Royal Collection

Page 45
• Joan Hassall, *Prince Charles's invitation to the Coronation*, 1953, watercolour, Collection of HRH The Prince of Wales, The Royal Collection © 2011, HM Queen Elizabeth II
• Model of the Coronation Coach, Johill Co., metal painted gold (RCIN 54036)
• *Coronation Procession of Her Majesty Queen Elizabeth II*, from *The Coronation of Her Majesty Queen Elizabeth II*, approved souvenir programme, 1953. Copyright Reserved/The Royal Collection

Page 46
• Queen Elizabeth II's gold Armills, 1952-3, Garrard (RCIN 31724)

Page 47
• Charles II's Coronation Regalia, 1661, Robert Vyner, gold, enamel, gems (RCIN 31732, 31723, 31717, 31713, 31712, 31700, 31718, 31725)

Page 48
• *Fireworks over Westminster and the Thames on the evening of the Coronation, 2 June 1953* (RCIN 2002708). Copyright Reserved/ The Royal Collection

Page 49
• *The Queen returning to Buckingham Palace wearing the Imperial State Crown and carrying the Orb and Sceptre, following the Coronation ceremony, 2 June 1953* (RCIN 2002719). Copyright Reserved/The Royal Collection

Page 50
• Evening dress, 1953, Norman Hartnell, gold lamé overlaid with cream lace and embroidered in gold thread (RCIN 200112)
• Wattle brooch, 1954, William Drummond & Co., Melbourne, diamonds (RCIN 250030)
• *The Queen at Flemington Racecourse, Melbourne, 1954* (RCIN 2506540). Copyright Reserved/The Royal Collection

Page 51
• Garter Star, 1923, diamonds and enamel (RCIN 200147)
• *The Queen in Garter Robes, November 1955*, photograph by Cecil Beaton (RCIN 2999982)
• The Marlborough Great George, 1825, diamonds, enamel, gold (RCIN 250075)

Page 52
• A.L. Wilcox, *HMY* Britannia *arriving at Tower Pier, London, May 1954*, oil on canvas (RCIN 402053). Collection of HRH The Duke of Edinburgh
• *The Royal Family on HMY* Britannia, *1956* (RCIN 500782). Copyright Reserved/The Royal Collection
• Sir Hugh Casson, *Corgis observing HMY* Britannia, from an illustrated letter, pen and ink and watercolour

Page 53
• *The Queen arriving at the House of Representatives, Lagos, 2 February 1956*, photograph by Stanley Devon (RCIN 2003058). The Times, London 02.02.1956
• Evening gown, 1956, Norman Hartnell, duchesse satin with embroidery of pearls, sequins and looped bugle beads (RCIN 200111)

Page 54
• *The Queen's car in Lower Broadway, New York, October 1957* (RCIN 2003331). Topfoto/Getty Images
• 'The Queen's Cup', 1957, Steuben, designed by George Thompson, engraving by Bruce Moore, glass (RCIN 63175)

Page 55
• *The Queen at her desk in Buckingham Palace, 25 January 1959* photograph: Topfoto/Getty Images
• Red dispatch box with EIIR insignia

Page 56
• The Duke of Edinburgh, *The Queen at the breakfast table in the private dining room, Windsor Castle, c.1960*, oil on canvas (RCIN 406980). Collection of HRH The Duke of Edinburgh

Page 57
• *The Queen with 'Sugar' at Frogmore, Windsor, May 1959*, photograph by Studio Lisa, Camera Press
• Marjorie Porter, *Sugar*, 1957, coloured chalks (RCIN 451863)
• Sir Hugh Casson, *Conference (snoozing corgis)*, from an illustrated letter, pen and ink and watercolour

Page 58
• *Queen Elizabeth II, The Duke of Edinburgh, Prince Charles, Princess Anne and Prince Andrew, 1960*, photograph by Cecil Beaton (RCIN 2943860)
• C. Day-Lewis, 'Birthday Song for a Royal Child', 1960 (RCIN 1047141.a)

Page 59
• Queen Mary's 'Lovers' Knot' brooch, late nineteenth century, diamonds, silver and gold (RCIN 200142)
• *The Queen seated at Buckingham Palace on the day of Princess Margaret's wedding, May 1960*, photograph by Cecil Beaton
• Turquoise dress and jacket, 1960, Norman Hartnell, ribbed silk and lace (RCIN 100041)

Page 60
• Invitation to banquet from the President of India to The Queen and The Duke of Edinburgh, 1961, box: dark wood decorated with gilt paint; invitation: bark (RCIN 92663.1.a-e)
• *The Queen riding a richly decorated elephant in Benares, 1961*, photograph by kind permission of Reginald Davis MBE
• *Princess Elizabeth and companions riding an elephant at London Zoo, 10 May 1939* (RCIN 2002142). Copyright Reserved/The Royal Collection

Page 61
• Graham Sutherland, *Design for 'Christ in Glory'*, 1954, coloured chalk and bodycolour (RCIN 451817). Collection of HRH The Duke of Edinburgh; Estate of Graham Sutherland
• *The Queen signing the Sentence of Consecration of Coventry Cathedral, 25 May 1962*, photograph by Greenwood (RCIN 2007621). The Times, London, 26.05.1962

Page 62
• *The Queen opening the New Zealand Parliament in Wellington, 18 February 1963*, photograph: Archives New Zealand/Te Rua Maara O Te Kāwanatanga Wellington Office and the Alexander Turnbull Library
• Dress worn by The Queen at the opening of the *New Zealand Parliament*, February 1963, photograph by Joe Little
• 'Budding Cloud' hand club, presented 1963, greenstone (RCIN 37065)

Page 63
- *The Queen with Prince Edward and the infant Prince Andrew, May 1964,* photograph by Cecil Beaton (RCIN 2999987)
- *Prince Edward's christening cake,* 1964 (RCIN 2999828)

Page 64
- *The Queen with Emperor Haile Selassie, February 1965* (RCIN 2003217). Copyright Reserved/The Royal Collection
- Evening gown, 1965, Norman Hartnell, silk shift with green sequin embroidery (RCIN 200122)
- Gilt and white metal cross, presented 1969 (RCIN 37028)

Page 65
- The Queen's programme and programme cover for the World Cup, 30 July 1966 (RA PS/QEII/PS 12800.34). Photograph: The Royal Collection; Copyright Reserved
- *The Queen presenting the World Cup to Bobby Moore, Wembley, 30 July 1966* (RCIN 2999827). S&G/EMPICS/Alpha

Page 66
- The Imperial State Crown, 1937, Garrard, gold and silver with gems (RCIN 31701)
- The Diamond Diadem, 1820, Rundell Bridge & Rundell, diamonds, pearls, silver and gold (RCIN 31702)
- *The Queen and The Duke of Edinburgh at the Palace of Westminster for the State Opening of Parliament, 15 November 2006,* photograph by Ian Jones

Page 67
- *The Queen reading her speech at the State Opening of Parliament, November 1967* (RCIN 2007455). Copyright Reserved/The Royal Collection

Page 68
- *The Queen dressed in her Admiral's cloak, October 1968,* photograph by Cecil Beaton (RCIN 2999826)
- *The Queen at the opening of the new Royal Mint at Llantrisant with the Deputy Master of the Mint, Jack James and the numismatic artist Christopher Ironside, December 1968,* photograph: courtesy of Media Wales Ltd.
- Coins (dated 1971) struck by The Prince of Wales (2p), The Queen (1p), and The Duke of Edinburgh (½p), 1968 (RCIN 443906, 443909, 443915). Crown Copyright

Page 69
- Blue wax seal attached to The Prince of Wales's letters patent (RA WARRANT/CPW/1958)
- *The Queen and The Prince of Wales at the investiture of The Prince of Wales, Caernarvon Castle, July 1969,* photograph by kind permission of Reginald Davis MBE
- Louis Osman, *The investiture coronet of The Prince of Wales,* 1969, gold, diamonds and emeralds (RCIN 69058)

Page 70
- *Aerial view of HMY* Britannia *escorted into Brisbane Harbour, April 1970* (RCIN 2003899). Copyright Reserved/The Royal Collection
- *The Queen in her Sitting Room at Buckingham Palace, 1970,* photograph by Joan Williams, BBC (RCIN 2999825)

Page 71
- Diamond-set Thistle Star, c.1820 (RCIN 200150)
- *The Queen in Thistle Robes before the Thistle Service in St Giles's Cathedral, July 1971,* photograph by Denis Straughan, The Scotsman Publications Ltd.
- Double-sided diamond-mounted Garter and Thistle Badge, cameo engraved by Edward Burch, c.1810, reset 1829 and 1840 (RCIN 100032v)

Page 72
- *The Queen with King Bhumibol during the State Visit to Thailand, February 1972* (RCIN 2999824). Copyright Reserved/The Royal Collection
- White evening gown, 1960, Norman Hartnell, crepe shift with yellow beaded embroidery (RCIN 100039)

Page 73
- *The Queen and The Duke of Edinburgh entering the City of London during their Silver Wedding celebrations, 20 November 1972* (RCIN 2999848). Copyright Reserved/The Royal Collection
- Gerald Benney, *Nest of silver boxes engraved with views of the royal residences,* 1972 (RCIN 95749)

Page 74
- *The Queen at the Maundy Service at Westminster Abbey, 19 April 1973,* photograph by kind permission of Reginald Davis MBE
- Order of Service for the Maundy Service at Westminster Abbey, 19 April 1973 (RA PS/QEII/PS 12800.49). Copyright The Dean & Chapter of Westminster, photograph © 2011 HM Queen Elizabeth II
- Silver Maundy Money including a set of four silver coins for 1973, Royal Mint (RCIN 443920). Crown Copyright

Page 75
- Roy Miller, *Highclere, with Joe Mercer up (wearing The Queen's colours),* 1974, oil on canvas (RCIN 401289)
- *The Queen in the winner's enclosure at Newmarket after Highclere had won the 1,000 Guineas, 1974,* photograph by Alec Russell
- The Queen's racing colours

Page 76
- The Order of Australia: Dame's badge, Royal Australian Mint, 1978 (RCIN 441549)
- The Order of Canada: Companion's badge, 1967 (RCIN 441545)
- The Queen's Service Order, New Zealand: Lady's Badge, 1975 (RCIN 441553)

Page 77
- Silver key to the Palace of Holyroodhouse, 1820, W. Marshall & Co. (RCIN 99052)
- *The Queen at the Tercentenary Parade of the Royal Company of Archers at the Palace of Holyroodhouse, Edinburgh, 19 October 1976,* photograph: The Royal Collection; reproduced by kind permission of The Queen's Bodyguard for Scotland (Royal Company of Archers)
- *The Archer's cup,* 1976, engraved by Alison Geissler, glass (RCIN 29045)

Page 78
- *The Queen at the Silver Jubilee Thanksgiving Service in St Paul's Cathedral, June 1977* (RCIN 2007275). Copyright Reserved/The Royal Collection
- Order of Service for the Thanksgiving Service at St Paul's Cathedral to celebrate the twenty-fifth anniversary of the accession of Queen Elizabeth II, 7 June 1977, reproduced by kind permission of the Dean of St Paul's Cathedral

Page 90
- *The Queen riding Burmese for the Birthday Parade, June 1985* (RCIN 2007076). Copyright Reserved/The Royal Collection
- Side-saddle used by The Queen when riding Burmese, 1969, Turner & Bridger, Epsom (RCIN 93813)
- Burmese's headcollar, c.1974-90 (RCIN 98010; detail)

Page 91
- *The Queen riding Burmese, with other members of the Royal Family, for the Birthday Parade, June 1978* (RCIN 2007292). Copyright Reserved/ The Royal Collection
- Plumed hat worn by The Queen for the Birthday Parade

Page 92
- *Sixtieth birthday portrait of The Queen, 1986,* photograph by The Duke of York (RCIN 502021). HRH Prince Andrew, Camera Press
- Graham Rust, *Design for a bookplate for The Queen,* 1986, pen and ink and wash (RCIN 452736)

Page 93
- *The Queen photographing The Duke of Edinburgh in China, October 1986* (RCIN 2002884). Copyright Reserved/The Royal Collection
- *The Queen inspecting the terracotta warriors at Xian, 16 October 1986,* photograph by Peter Bregg, PA/EMPICS

Page 94
- Letter patent, with royal sign manual, granting the title of Princess Royal to The Princess Anne, 9 June 1987 (RA Warrants/ASPR). The Royal Archives; Crown Copyright material reproduced with the permission of the Crown Office of the House of Lords; photograph © 2011 HM Queen Elizabeth II

Page 95
- Selection of nine Christmas cards sent by The Queen and Duke of Edinburgh, 1985-2002 (RCIN 2999883, 2999877, 2999881, 2999879, 2999880, 2999882, 29999874, 29999878, 29999875). Copyright Reserved/The Royal Collection
- Sir Hugh Casson, *Father Christmas with reindeer,* from an illustrated letter, watercolour and pen and ink

Page 96
- Fragment of the Berlin Wall, demolished 1989 (RCIN 37064)
- *The Queen and President Gorbachev of the USSR during his visit to Windsor Castle, April 1989,* photograph courtesy of Baylis Media Ltd.
- Notice sheet concerning President Gorbachev's visit, 7 April 1989 © 2011, HM Queen Elizabeth II

Page 97
- *The Queen visiting the hot springs at Krisuvik, Iceland, 27 June 1990* (RCIN 2880511). Copyright Reserved/The Royal Collection
- The Icelandic Government's printed programme for the State Visit to Iceland, June 1990, © 2011, HM Queen Elizabeth II

Page 98
- *The Queen addressing a meeting of both Houses of Congress, 16 May 1991,* photograph by Anwar Hussein
- *'Shakespeare' flower bowl,* Steuben, designed by Jane Osborn-Smith, glass, presented 1991 (RCIN 95751)
- Programme for the State Visit to Washington DC, May 1991, © 2011, HM Queen Elizabeth II

Page 99
- Ted Hughes, 'The Unicorn', 6 February 1992 (RCIN 1008643). Poem © Estate of Ted Hughes, photograph: The Royal Collection

Page 100
- Stained glass window in the new Private Chapel, Windsor Castle, completed 1997, Joseph Nuttgens, to a design by The Duke of Edinburgh
- *The north-east corner of the Quadrangle, Windsor Castle ablaze, 20 November 1992,* photograph by Tim Graham, Getty Images
- *The Queen with a fireman at Windsor Castle, 20 November 1992,* photograph courtesy of the Royal Berkshire Fire and Rescue Services

Page 101
- *Opening day queues for Buckingham Palace line The Mall, 7 August 1993,* photograph by Fiona Hanson, PA
- Buckingham Palace Summer Opening souvenir mug and tickets, 1993
- *Hungary's President Arpad Goncz with Queen Elizabeth II and the Duke of Edinburgh in Budapest's Parliament Square for the official welcome of the Royal couple to Hungary for a four-day state visit, 1993,* photograph by Martin Keene, PA

Page 102
- Coloured lace ribbon with gilt medal commemorating the inauguration of the Channel Tunnel, 6 May 1994 (RCIN 63720, 446152)
- *The Queen and President Mitterand of France at the official opening of the Channel Tunnel, May 1994,* photograph by Tim Ockenden (RCIN 28999999). PA/EMPICS

Page 103
- *The Queen with Queen Elizabeth The Queen Mother and Princess Margaret on the balcony of Buckingham Palace, on the fiftieth anniversary of VE Day, 8 May 1995,* photograph by Stewart Mark, Camera Press
- *The Royal Family with Winston Churchill on the balcony of Buckingham Palace, VE Day, 8 May 1945* (RCIN 2999895). ILN, Camera Press

Page 104
- *The Queen and Nelson Mandela, President of South Africa, before the State Banquet at Buckingham Palace, July 1996,* WPA Rota photograph by John Stillwell PA/EMPICS
- Programme for the State Banquet for President Mandela, 9 July 1996 © 2011 HM Queen Elizabeth II
- Sarah Mackie, *Silk head scarf,* 1996 (RCIN 94158)

Page 105
- *The Queen and The Duke of Edinburgh outside Buckingham Palace among the tributes to Diana, Princess of Wales, September 1997,* photograph by Camera Press

Page 106
- *The Queen and The Duke of Edinburgh, with members of the Royal Family, at the Thanksgiving Service for the Golden Wedding, Westminster Abbey, November 1997,* photograph by John Sillwell, PA/EMPICS
- Glass martini jug with E and P overlaid in gold around neck, 1997 (RCIN 95750)

Page 107
• Programme for The Queen's Reception for
The Prince of Wales, 13 November 1998,
© 2011, HM Queen Elizabeth II
• *The Queen and The Prince of Wales at the
reception for his fiftieth birthday at Buckingham
Palace, 13 November 1998*, photograph by
Camera Press

Page 108
• *The Queen inspecting a model of the Millennium
Dome during a visit to the Royal Institution of
Chartered Surveyors in London, 29 July 1999*,
photograph by Scan Dempsey, PA/EMPICS
• *The Queen at Greenwich, after lighting the
millennium flame, 31 December 1999*,
photograph by Fiona Hanson, PA/EMPICS

Page 109
• *Queen Elizabeth The Queen Mother and
The Queen on the balcony of Buckingham Palace
on Queen Elizabeth's hundredth birthday, 4 August
2000*, photograph by Jeff Moore (RCIN
2999977). National Pictures
• Congratulatory telegram, with envelope, sent by
The Queen to Queen Elizabeth on her hun-
dredth birthday, 4 August 2000 (RA
QEQM/PRIV/CSP/FAM)

Page 110
• EIIR finishing tool used in the Royal Bindery,
Windsor (RCIN 98011)
• *The Queen exchanging gifts at the Vatican with
Pope John Paul II, October 2000*, photograph:
PA/EMPICS

Page 111
• *The Queen at the Remembrance Day service,
Whitehall, November 2001*, photograph by Toby
Melville, PA/EMPICS

Page 112
• Order of Service for the funeral of Princess
Margaret at St George's Chapel, Windsor, 15
February 2002 © 2011, HM Queen Elizabeth II
• Order of Service for the funeral of Queen
Elizabeth The Queen Mother at Westminster
Abbey, 9 April 2002, Copyright The Dean and
Chapter of Westminster, photograph: The Royal
Collection
• Alexander Creswell, *The lying-in-state of
Queen Elizabeth The Queen Mother in Westminster
Hall in April 2002*, watercolour and bodycolour
(RCIN 933811)

Page 113
• *The Queen in her Golden Jubilee Year, 2002*,
photograph by Mark Lawrence, copyright
www.royalimages.co.uk
• The Grand Duchess Vladimir's diamond tiara,
set with pearls, c.1874, attributed to Bolin,
St Petersburg (RCIN 200145)
• The Queen's Family Order of King George VI,
red enamel and diamonds (RCIN 200167)
• The Queen's Family Order of King George V,
red enamel and diamonds (RCIN 200166)

Page 114
• Programme, plan of Buckingham Palace
Gardens and tickets for the Golden Jubilee
concerts at Buckingham Palace, June 2002
• *The Queen meets Sir Paul McCartney, Sir Cliff
Richard and other performers on stage in the
gardens of Buckingham Palace, 3 June 2002*,
photograph by Stefan Rousseau, PA
• *'Queen' guitarist Brian May plays the national
anthem from the roof of Buckingham Palace at the
start of the second Golden Jubilee concert, 3 June
2002*, photograph by Stefan Rousseau, PA

Page 115
• *The Queen in the Gold State Coach travelling to
St Paul's Cathedral for the service of Thanksgiving
to celebrate her Golden Jubilee, 4 June 2002*,
photograph: PA
• *George III's State Coach, c.1762*, engraving after
John Linnell (RCIN 504026)
• *The Queen and The Duke of Edinburgh watch
Concorde fly past from the balcony of Buckingham
Palace, 4 June 2002*, photograph: PA

Page 116
• Paul Sandby, *South-east view of Windsor Castle
from the Home Park, c.1765*, bodycolour on
panel, acquired 1978 (RCIN 918986)
• Basin, cover and stand with Stuart royal arms,
c.1748-52, Vincennes, soft-paste porcelain, basin
and cover acquired 1964, stand acquired 1997
(RCIN 19605)
• Caddinet, Anthony Nelme, silver-gilt, 1688-9,
acquired 1975 (RCIN 31736)
• French psalter with poem signed by Elizabeth I,
c.1520, wedding present, 1947 (RCIN 1051596)
• Lucian Freud, *Queen Elizabeth II, 1999-2001*,
oil on canvas, presented by the artist in 2001
(RCIN 407895). The Royal Collection © Lucian
Freud
• Queen Mary's patch box, c.1694, gold, enamel,
diamonds, acquired 1963 (RCIN 19133)
• John Hoskins, *Queen Henrietta Maria, c.1632*,
watercolour and bodycolour on vellum, acquired
1968 (RCIN 420891)

Page 117
• *The Prince of Wales and The Queen at the
opening of The Queen's Gallery, Buckingham
Palace, May 2002*, Copyright Reserved/
The Royal Collection

Page 118
• *The Queen and Prince William on the balcony at
Buckingham Palace, June 2003*, photograph by
Anwar Hussein, PA/EMPICS
• *Golden Jubilee equestrian monument to
The Queen in Windsor Great Park, February 2006*,
photograph by The Duke of Edinburgh (RCIN
2999819). Copyright Reserved/The Royal
Collection

Page 119
• *The Queen riding at Windsor with Zara Phillips
and The Princess Royal, 10 April 2004*, photograph
by Eva Zielinska-Millar (RCIN 2999907)
• *The Queen riding at Ascot, June 1960* (RCIN
2006975). Copyright Reserved/The Royal
Collection

Page 120
• *The Queen, The Duke of Edinburgh and the
Princess Royal with members of the International
Olympic Committee in the Music Room at
Buckingham Palace, February 2005*, photograph
by Kirsty Wigglesworth, PA
• *The Queen in St George's Hall, Windsor Castle,
at the reception following the Thanksgiving Service
for the marriage of The Prince of Wales and
The Duchess of Cornwall, 9 April 2005*,
photograph by Hugo Burnand
• Order of Service for the Thanksgiving Service
at St George's Chapel, Windsor Castle, for
the marriage of The Prince of Wales and
The Duchess of Cornwall, 9 April 2005
• Decorative tin box containing a piece of the
cake made to celebrate the marriage of
The Prince of Wales and The Duchess of
Cornwall, 2005

Page 121
• Order of Service for the London 2005 Service
of Remembrance at St Paul's Cathedral,
1 November 2005, reproduced by kind
permission of the Dean of St Paul's Cathedral
• *Margaret Thatcher greets The Queen on her
arrival at Lady Thatcher's eightieth birthday
celebrations at the Mandarin Oriental Hotel,
London, 13 October 2005*, photograph:
© Reuters/Kieran Doherty
• *The Queen watches a flypast of RAF Jaguars
during her visit to RAF Coltishall, Norfolk, 17
November 2005*, photograph by Arthur Edwards,
MBE, © The Sun

Page 122
• *The Queen looking through her eightieth birthday cards, 2006,* photograph by Fiona Hanson, PA
• Gordon Rushmer, *Royal birthday card from the Sea Rangers,* 2006, watercolour (RCIN 934017)
• Margaret Scott, *Royal birthday card with residences and wildlife,* 2006, watercolour (RCIN 934016)

Page 123
• *Eightieth birthday portrait of HM The Queen, February 2006,* photograph by Jane Bown (RCIN 2999843). Camera Press

Page 124
• *The Queen and The Duke of Edinburgh attend a Service of Thanksgiving for The Queen's eightieth birthday at St Paul's Cathedral, London, 15 June 2006,* photograph by Ian Jones
• *The Queen with Postman Pat and Jess at the Children's Garden Party at Buckingham Palace, June 2006,* photograph: PA
• Programme for the Children's Garden Party at Buckingham Palace, 25 June 2006

Page 125
• *The Queen and The Duke of Edinburgh joined at Clarence House by members of their family to celebrate their Diamond Wedding Anniversary, November 2007,* photograph by Tim Graham, PA Wire
• *The Queen and The Duke of Edinburgh greet couples who share their sixtieth wedding anniversary, 19 November 2007,* photograph by Kieran Doherty, PA Wire
• Order of Service, Diamond Wedding Anniversary of The Queen and The Duke of Edinburgh, Westminster Abbey, 19 November 2007, copyright The Dean and Chapter of Westminster

Page 126
• *The Queen at the opening ceremony of Commonwealth Heads of Government Meeting (CHOGM) in the Ugandan capital Kampala, 23 November 2007,* photograph by Chris Radburn, WPA Rota/PA Wire
• Brooch in the form of a spray of sorghum, gold and diamonds, presented 2007 (RCIN 250037)
• Glass bottle containing water from the River Nile, presented 2007 (RCIN 95971). Copyright Reserved/The Royal Collection
• Black glazed pottery vase, presented 2007 (RCIN 95991)

Page 127
• *The Queen and the French President, Nicolas Sarkozy, arrive for the State Banquet at Windsor Castle, 26 March 2008,* photograph by Carl de Souza, PA Wire
• Ruby and diamond tiara, 1973, Garrard

Page 128
• *Group photograph at Frogmore House following the marriage of Peter Phillips and Autumn Kelly, 17 May 2008,* photograph by Sir Geoffrey Shakerley, PA Wire
• *The Royal Family in the gardens of Frogmore House, 1965* (RCIN 2937883)

Page 129
• The Commonwealth Mace, 1992, gold, silver-gilt and enamel (RCIN 250043)
• *The Queen is greeted by children dressed in carnival costumes at The Queen's Centre, Port of Spain, Trinidad, 28 November 2009,* photograph by Chris Radburn, PA Wire
• *The Queen is presented with a football from Dwight Yorke and a signed cricket bat from Brian Lara during a reception at the Carlton Savana Hotel, Port of Spain, Trinidad, 28 November 2009,* photograph by Chris Radburn, PA Wire
• *Cricket bat, presented 2009* (RCIN 99559). Copyright Reserved/The Royal Collection

Page 130
• *The Queen with recipients of The Elizabeth Cross, Catterick, September 2009,* photograph by J. Barron MoD, Newspix International
• The Elizabeth Cross, 2009 (RCIN 441960)

Page 131
• Maple-leaf brooch, 1939, Asprey & Co., platinum and diamonds (RCIN 250031)
• *The Queen during the royal tour of Canada, 2010,* photograph: Department of Canadian Heritage, 2010; Reproduced with the permission of the Minister of Public Works and Government Services Canada, 2011 © Her Majesty The Queen in Right of Canada (2010)

Page 132
• *The Queen addressing the United Nations in New York, 6 July 2010,* photograph: © Reuters/Mike Segar
• Pair of aquamarine and diamond clips, Boucheron, presented 1944 (RCIN 200135.1-2)

Page 133
• *Group photograph at Buckingham Palace following the marriage of Prince William and Catherine Middleton, 29 April 2011,* photograph by Hugo Burnand, © St James's Palace
• Queen Elizabeth's Halo Tiara, Cartier, 1936, diamonds and platinum

Page 134
• *The Queen arrives for the State Banquet at Dublin Castle, 18 May 2011,* photograph by Anwar Hussein, EMPICS Entertainment
• Queen Mary's 'Girls of Great Britain' tiara, 1893, E. Wolff & Co. for Garrard, diamonds and silver (RCIN 200192)

Page 135
• R.T. Pritchett, *Queen Victoria's Diamond Jubilee Garden Party at Buckingham Palace, 28 June 1897,* watercolour (RCIN 920902)
• The official Diamond Jubilee emblem, designed in 2011 by ten-year-old Catherine Dewar of Chester. It was the winner of a competition hosted by the BBC television programme Blue Peter.
• Silver strut frame with two portraits of Queen Victoria including the official 1897 Diamond Jubilee portrait by W. & D. Downey, 1897-8 (RCIN 52465)

Page 136
• *The Queen on horseback at Windsor with her youngest grandchildren, Viscount Severn and Lady Louise Windsor, 25 April 2011,* photograph by Eva Zielinska-Millar, © HM Queen Elizabeth II

Page 137
• Cream silk gown, 1950s?, Norman Hartnell (RCIN 200120)

Page 138
• Diamond Jubilee medals, Crown Copyright/MOD 2011

Page 141
• Evening coat, 1970s, Norman Hartnell, embroidered silver tulle edged with fur (RCIN 200130)

Page 142
• White leather handbag, 1970, Launer

Every effort has been made to contact copyright holders; any omissions are inadvertent and will be corrected in future editions if notification of the amended credit is sent to the Publisher in writing.

Written by Jane Roberts. Published by Royal Collection Trust / © HM Queen Elizabeth II 2012.

First published 2011. This edition reprinted 2012.

013894

ISBN 978 1 905686 40 7

British Library Cataloguing in Publication Data:
A catalogue record for this book is available from the British Library

Designed by Peter Drew of Phrogg Design
Typeset in Garamond
Printed and bound by Studio Fasoli, Verona
Printed on Symbol Tatami White, Fedrigoni Cartiere Spa, Verona
Production by Debbie Wayment

Endpapers:
Graham Rust, *Design for a bookplate for The Queen*, 1986
(pen and ink and wash; RCIN 452736)

Title page:
Queen Victoria's Diamond Jubilee brooch, 1897,
R & S Garrard & Co., diamonds, pearls, silver, gold

Right:
Queen Mary II's Orb, 1689, Robert Vyner II,
rock, crystal, imitation gems, gold and silver (RCIN 31719)

MIX
Paper from
responsible sources
FSC® C018568

Find out more about
the Royal Collection at
www.royalcollection.org.uk